Don't Squeeze the Turtle
Tales from an Online Classroom

JINNY ALEXANDER

Copyright © Jinny Alexander 2025

Jinny Alexander has asserted her right to be identified as the author of this Work in accordance with the Copyright, Designs and Patents Act 1988

All rights reserved.

No part of this publication may be reproduced, distributed, or transmitted in any form or by any means, including photocopying, recording, or other electronic or mechanical methods, without the prior written permission of the publisher, except as permitted by copyright law.

ISBN Paperback: 978-1-916814-16-5

ISBN ebook: 978-1-916814-17-2

Cover Design: Wicked Good Book Covers

Cover Artwork and Chapter headers: aileemarieart

Visit www.jinnyalexander.com

This book is for my students. Every single one of them. Thank you for the fun you bring to my life.

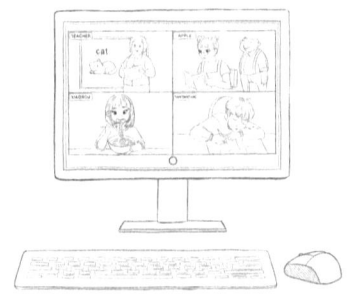

Contents

Introduction	1
Chinese names vs English names	8
January	12
February	45
March	73
April	101
May	130
June	154
July	166
August	185
September	209
And then what happened?	222
Seventy-four Days in Wuhan	226

Introduction

Nothing should really surprise me in this job, so a few weeks ago, when I found myself uttering the phrase, "Please take the mushroom out of your ear," I thought little of it.

A week later, I had a totally ridiculous hour-long lesson with the same student, that centred around all the ways the European Onion could save the world.

"What's the European Onion?" you might ask.

Indeed.

Mumu (aged seven, from China) and I were reading an article about data protection, and the measures the European Union has put in place. Let's not get into why a seven-year-old is studying a textbook aimed at university-age students. We'll save that for later. Overall, Mumu's reading is excellent, but on that day, he misread *European Union* for *European Onion* and it all started from there. For the rest of the lesson, our university-age content descended into a lesson far better suited to a seven-year-old. The European Onion, although it originated somewhere in Europe, as its name implies, has the ability to fly itself around the world, in or out of a frying pan, and solve all the problems you can imagine and probably many you can't. You know how onions make you cry? Well, I was crying with laughter. My favourite kind of lesson.

If you're still wondering about the mushroom, it has fewer humanitarian skills and ambitions than the European Onion, but attends class regularly. It's a confident class member and loves to be on camera. It fills the screen with its close-up presence, and demands I engage fully with it. It's remarkably knowledgeable, to be fair, for a red-and-white stuffed mushroom toy from a Mario Brothers game, and often, it doesn't leave *mushroom*[1] for Mumu to speak. Sometimes, it's replaced by one of Mumu's other toys. Jerry the Mouse is a regular attendee, for example, but he only ever wants to talk about Tom. A large plastic watermelon pops in from time to time, too, but it's not particularly chatty.

Of course, I have many more students than Mumu and his collection of toys, and many more amusing moments. During a university workshop a few years ago, we were tasked with writing two truths and one lie. These were mine:

---

1. Sorry. How could I not?

Over the heads of two giggling girls in Saudi Arabia, hangs a wide mirror. Reflected in the mirror, their mother—grandmother? I can't be sure, but there is definitely some sagging—strips from the waist up, unclips her bra, swings her breasts at someone unseen, then redresses herself.

In a Korean nightclub, my conversational adult student needs to pee. It's dark, so luckily I see little, but I've become more attuned to sound since doing this job. A clunk and flash of light indicate I'm lying on the stall floor, facing the ceiling. There's rustling, then a flush. I'm scooped from the floor and we're at the sinks. Raised, male voices exchange words I can't guess at, over a soundtrack of running water, or peeing. There's a scrape of a door, and her attention is on me once more. She giggles, embarrassed not by putting me through the whole toilet experience, but only by the fact she accidentally used the men's toilets.

In China, seven-year-old Jacob focuses intently on our class; all his attention on me and his classmate, Cat. Behind Jacob, his little brother—often a presence and source of background entertainment—scales a shelving unit. I call frantic warnings, but my student brushes them off: "It's nothing. He is just trouble," and the shelf topples slowly forward.[2]

---

2. The lie will be revealed at the end of the book. You'll find many more truths along the way.

I've worked in Early Childhood Education for over thirty years, and have been teaching English as a Second Language (ESL) online for the last eight years. When I began, I met with students in Brazil, Peru, Oman, Saudi Arabia, India, China, Japan, Italy, South Korea, Taiwan, France, and probably many other places I've long-forgotten. As time went by, I refined my classes to focus mainly on Chinese students, and mainly children.

Currently, I *only* teach children, and they are all in China or Romania. Sometimes I miss the variety, but the Chinese, at least for now, pay well and suit my timezone. Their after-school hours are my mornings, going into the early afternoon in summertime but finishing by 1 P.M. in winter hours. The Romanian classes are occasional and cover other teachers' leave or crises, and fit neatly into my afternoons, to dovetail with the Chinese hours.

At first, I worked for large online ESL companies, with regimented curricula and inflexible policies and unrealistic demands. In summer 2021, a change in the Chinese regulations crashed the online ESL industry literally overnight. Many of the large, established companies folded, and thousands of teachers were left without a job.

I was lucky. I moved into private classes with students I kept in contact with after the industry imploded. My reputation also gained me entry into smaller, better companies that had survived or dodged the Chinese government restrictions. Suddenly I was paid a better hourly rate, had more freedom to adapt lesson materials to suit the students' abilities, and a proper working relationship with the people I worked for, including getting to know students and parents in conversations beyond the classroom.

No longer just a cog in the machine of the bigger companies, I now have a flexibility and respect I really enjoy. And an endless source of inspiration, funny moments, and countless glimpses into other people's homes; other cultures, and the world beyond my cozy, book-lined office in rural Ireland.

Back in 2023, following that 'two truths, one lie' game, I kept a diary of my classes for about nine months. The mushroom-in-Mumu's-ear and the European Onion conversation reminded me of that diary — that record of many more funny, sometimes eye-opening, sometimes poignant moments — so I hunted down the file and, for the first time since writing it, read it through. What follows is that diary. I've tidied up typos, and rearranged some entries into chronological class order, and added a few footnotes to give details of books referred to or follow-up comments to record something that happened as a result of that day's entry. Aside from those small edits, it's unabridged and as it was written at the time.

Welcome to my world of online English classes.

Some notes regarding terminology:

I refer to classes as *private* or *company* throughout the diary. A company class is one arranged for me and paid for through an ESL (English as a Second Language) company. A private class is one I arrange through direct contact with the student or their parents.

Throughout the diary, my Chinese classes are often referred to in terms of BJT. This is Beijing Standard Time, and the entire country of China, despite spanning several lines of longitude, uses BJT. BJT is either seven or eight hours ahead of my timezone: GMT (Greenwich Mean Time), depending on the time of year. In China, there are no clock changes for summertime, so in summer, my Chinese classes tend to run between 9 A.M. and 2 P.M. GMT+1 (or British Summer Time) and in winter, from 8 A.M. until 1 P.M. GMT.

Some lessons are referred to in terms such as GKA, G1B, etc. These are loosely linked to USA school grades, so a G1 lesson is aimed at children with a Grade 1 level of English. G = Grade. K = Kindergarten. A and B refer to the two half-levels of each grade, thus GKA is followed by GKB, then G1A, and so on.

Chinese names vs English names

A teacher of English as a Second Language is likely to meet a lot of students, often from many different countries and cultures, and each one bringing aspects of that culture into the classroom — that's one of the best parts of the job.

This, of course, means we see many different names. In most cultures, the student comes to class with their given name; the name used by their friends and family.

With Chinese students, it's less straightforward. Many Chinese students adopt an English name to use in their English classes. Often they choose this name, or have it chosen for them, when they first begin their English-learning journey. Some teachers I know insist their students use an English name, even going so far as to bestow an English name upon a child. I do not. (In fact, I am strongly opposed to this practice and find it culturally and morally inappropriate. I also firmly believe that if a child can come to class for an hour or more every week to learn my language, the very least I can do is to learn their name.) Thus, despite the hilarity it usually ensues, I do my best to learn a student's Chinese name, even if this is not the name we use in class. With some, I rely heavily on writing the name phonetically on a Post-it®, stuck to the edge of my screen until I get it right. With some, I never quite get to grips with the pronunciation, but it is a good reminder for me of how hard it must be for my students to master certain words in English.

Therefore, in this diary, you will see a mix of Chinese names (in their Romanised form, which is what we use in class); English names, and what at first appear to be the names of random objects, but are, in fact, the student's chosen name.

Some students change their name from time to time. This might be because they haven't yet chosen an English name and are still trying different names for size, searching for one they like. Some may have outgrown a 'baby' name and want to choose a name more suited to a high-schooler or adult (such as NIMO becoming CRAIG).

Some change their name simply because they are Tiantian. Tiantian does not appear in the months covered in this diary, but was a funny and delightful 6-year-old, bursting with energy and bringing oodles of laughter to every class. I taught Tiantian for about two years, including through seventy-four days of Covid lockdown, confined to a small apartment in Wuhan, while his mother grew visibly more fraught with each week that passed.[1] Tiantian took great delight in adding an extra 'tian' to his name for several consecutive weeks. In that particular ESL company, feedback was only accepted by the automated system if the student name typed into the feedback form exactly matched the name on the record for that day. Over a few weeks, I painstakingly entered TIANTIANTIAN, then TIANTIANTIANTIAN, then TIANTIANTIANTIANTIAN, and onwards, until he finally gave up and appeared as SPIDERMAN instead.

It is particularly common for young students to pick names of popular Disney characters. At one point, I had five ELSAS and four ERICS on my weekly schedule. Fruit names are also popular, and I've had APPLE, CHERRY, and MANGO, to name some. We also see boys choosing names that are more typical as girls' names, and vice versa. I have taught boys named SKY and SUMMER, and boys and girls called SUNNY. Some of my colleagues have reported names far more obscure than those belonging to any of my students. My most unusual to date are probably ONLY and CARROT, but it's surprising how quickly they become a 'name' rather than a 'word'.

---

1. See page 226 for a flash fiction piece, *Seventy-four Days in Wuhan*, based on this experience. A shortened version of this piece was long-listed for the Bath Flash Fiction Award in 2022 and is featured in ***Dandelion Years, Bath Flash Fiction Volume Seven*, Ad Hoc Fiction, 2022 (ISBN 978-1-915247-10-0)**

Throughout this diary, I have used the actual names used by the students in each class. It seemed more authentic and appropriate than making up a random list comprised of Chinese names, English names, and names generated by miscellaneous objects. Besides, without these students, there would be no diary, so it seems only fair to attribute them. They, after all, are the inspiration and the story.

January

SUNDAY JANUARY 1, 2023
NUMBER OF CLASSES: 0
LESSONS TO PLAN: 1

Today is both a Sunday and a holiday, so I've no classes.

In an ideal world, I wouldn't be working at all, but in real life, I didn't finish my lesson prep for the coming week. Two of my private classes have chosen to do a new literature course, both of which begin this week. I'm excited about this and really looking forward to these classes but the flip side is that I need to create entire courses from scratch for each one.

Harry and Susie (who are reuniting as classmates after about a year) are going to study *James and the Giant Peach*[1], yay! I already made their first lesson last week, and I'm delighted with

---

1. Dahl, R, *James and the Giant Peach*, Penguin, 1961

it both in terms of content and in how it looks visually on the screen. Making lessons is time-consuming, but fun.

Mango and Catherine are going to study *Wonder*[2]. I have reservations about this as it's a big jump from the level of reading they've done to this point. Catherine's mum has 'insisted', despite my suggestions to start with something a little easier, and I hope they can cope. Luckily the chapters are very short, which will make it less intimidating. I hadn't read the book – the film made me cry a lot, but Owen Wilson: yum. Catherine and Mango haven't seen the film and I'm not sure if it would help them to watch it first or not. That's not my decision, anyway.

Meanwhile, I've been reading the first chapters. I'd hoped to read the whole book over the Christmas break, but juggling that with *James and the Giant Peach* and some not-work reading that I really wanted to get done, and all the other things that eat into 'let's relax, it's Christmas' left me short of time, as always. It also seemed sensible to plan the comprehension-check questions as I read through *Wonder*, and take notes on each chapter, so I've only read the first fifteen pages or so, so far. I've my feet up on the coffee table, mindless TV on in the background, and I've just finished creating the first lesson. It only covers the first two chapters, because it

---

2. Palacio, R J, *Wonder*, Penguin Random House, 2012

also introduces the book, includes two different book trailers, and factors in time for the students to create their own blurb. As with my Lesson 1 for *James and the Giant Peach*, I'm delighted with how it looks and what it will cover. I'll be teaching *Wonder* on Tuesday, and the *James and the Giant Peach* Lesson 1 on Wednesday, so it won't be much of a wait to see how they go and how the students react/cope.

That's my work done for today. I've one last day of no classes before the holidays are over, although I'll need to check whether I need to prep my other Tuesday classes tomorrow. Not doing it now – the evening demands relaxing with dinner and film. Happy New Year, everyone.

Monday January 2, 2023
Number of classes: 0
Lessons to plan for tomorrow: 0

I am better organised than I hoped. My other lessons for tomorrow are already planned and checked. I did them before the Christmas break, and this feels like a win.

Tuesday January 3, 2023
Number of classes: 4
Number of students: 1+3+4+2
Lessons to plan for tomorrow: 1

I'm up before daylight and not ready for it.

I eat a bowl of porridge in front of the computer while I set up my classes for the day. I skim through the two company classes to check what it is I'll be teaching today, and log onto the platform for my first student.

This first lesson is not really a lesson – it's a conversational platform, bringing native English speakers together with students worldwide and it pays next to nothing. It's where I started out in my ESL career, and in the beginning I met eight, ten, twelve students a day for anything between a few minutes to an hour or more at a time. It's a lazy option as it involves no preparation – the students are usually not studying any kind of set lesson, although over the years, the company has evolved and there are now some lessons available, but they are pretty rubbish and I avoid using them at all costs. Nowadays, I only meet a tiny handful of students on this platform, amounting to about seven 30-minute sessions a week with four different children. All of these are students I have known for several years, and I meet them because I like them, not for the money.

Today, it's a 9 A.M. meeting with Dorrie, who had her birthday while I was away and has just turned thirteen.

When I log on, the platform offers me a '2022 round up' which informs me I've been using this platform for five and a half years. This means I've known Dorrie since she was seven. When we first met, she was a complete beginner. I sat in my kitchen, showing her different vegetables from my fridge, and teaching her 'big, bigger, biggest' and other such basics.

Today, we are partway through the second Harry Potter[3] book. We finished the first one in the summer, and it took us about two years to read it – 30 minutes twice a week, with chat and comprehension checks along the way. This second one has harder vocabulary in it, so after speeding up towards the end of Book 1, we've slowed down again, but Dorrie's comprehension of the story is great. She's seen the films, of course, which helps.

Next, I have two classes with the Chinese company I work for, then one private. I'm looking forward to the private one most – our first *Wonder* class – although my first company class on a Tuesday is always nice, too.

---

3. Rowling, J. K, *Harry Potter and the Chamber of Secrets*, Bloomsbury, 1998

In the final class of the day, it takes a while for Catherine and Mango to get into the Zoom room, so we start ten minutes late.

I task them with writing a short (one or two paragraphs max) blurb for the book, using information from the two trailer videos we watched, but I already know the biggest issue we'll have with studying *Wonder* is not related to its content or difficulty, but the age-old issue I have with this pair of students: they always want to write too much. I can tell they are trying to summarize the entire story, despite not having read it yet.

Catherine, whose mum pushed us to study this book, has already ploughed ahead and has filled in a lot of her character profiles before we started, which is both helpful and unhelpful. It leaves her classmate, Mango, behind before we start, and makes it much harder to do a chapter-by-chapter study as per my newly-made lesson plans, but it does help her understand the greater story.

In my first company class, Honey (who has a writing class on Tuesdays and a literature class on Wednesdays) reminds me of just how much prep I need to put in this afternoon to get tomorrow's literature class ready. We're reading a great book, but it has LOOOONNNG chapters, and I need to read the next five AND make a lesson to go with them. I love love love this literature course, but I could do with dedicating the afternoon to my MA work, not reading a middle grade book.

Today's true highlight comes in the second of my company classes, where Kayley, not knowing the corrrect word, refers to mermaids as "beautiful people-fish."

WEDNESDAY JANUARY 4, 2023
NUMBER OF CLASSES: 5
NUMBER OF STUDENTS: 1+3+2+1+1
LESSONS TO PLAN FOR TOMORROW: 1

The day starts with Dorrie, who I don't usually meet on a Wednesday, but the bank holiday shifted us on a day this week. I remember she would have had different classes at school from the usual Monday and Tuesday ones she tells me about, and get her to tell me about those. She tells me she had a sewing class. Last week, they learned to sew on a button. We crack on with Harry Potter and today the words I decide I need to explain for Dorrie are *pummelled*, *accelerator*, *plunged*, and *glove compartment*. Any Harry Potter fans will know which section of the story we've got to. I wasn't sure if she knew what toffees are (you know, the ones in the bag in the glove compartment, that sustain Harry and Ron as they fly the car to Hogwarts), so I asked her.

"Do you know what a toffee is?"

"I think so," she said. "It's a... it's a thing!"

Why, yes, Dorrie, you are absolutely right.

In today's afternoon lesson with Buse, we merely hurl Shakespearean insults uponst each other's ears. Whole conversations in archaic words that hav'st meaning none, forthwith.

Thursday January 5, 2023
Number of classes: 3
Number of students: 3+2+3
Lessons to plan for tomorrow: 1

In the first of today's classes, Luna is typically angry, but it's not me or my class she hates today, so that's progress.

In the second class, Craig has decided that he doesn't know enough about David Beckham to write a biography on him, so he hasn't done any written work since our last class, despite having already 'false-started' and having been told to get on with it as it needed to be finished by today. He has, however, decided that he knows a lot about Pele. Indeed, he does, and I'm impressed, even in the absence of any written work. When I say, "He just died recently, didn't he?", Craig replies that yes, Pele died yesterday's yesterday's yesterday's yesterday. I lost count of the number of yesterdays, but he's probably spot on – it was six days ago. I should probably teach him it's quicker to just give the date, or to round it up to 'last week'. Kevin's biography subject has been dead a bit longer – he was a famous man I know only as "that Chinese Emperor you are writing about" because I still have no idea what the dude's name was. He lived and died in the 1300s, which is more yesterdays than anyone tries to count, even Kevin.

In the last class of the day, I make the mistake of asking Luffy, Cynthia, and Vincent what kind of robot they'd like to make. Cynthia doesn't want to make a robot. At first. However, once Luffy and Vincent plan the invention of increasingly violent human-killing machines, she joins in. Luckily, it's time to end the class, so I tell them their robots sound horrid and leave them with the explicit homework instruction to reread the text but to not ever build a robot, say "Go away," and end the lesson.

FRIDAY JANUARY 6, 2023
NUMBER OF CLASSES: 5
NUMBER OF STUDENTS: 2+2+4+1+1
LESSONS TO PLAN FOR MONDAY: 0

Today starts badly. I only have 2 classes scheduled for this morning, and am enjoying a little bit of a lie in, as the first class isn't until 10 A.M.. As usual, when I wake at about 8.30, I check my phone for class updates. Often there may be some feedback from the day before, or a cancelling student. Today's message 'reminds' me that a class will 'continue' at 8 P.M. Beijing time, today (12 noon my time). This is not a continuing class. The students scheduled are those from a trial on a Wednesday way back in November – so no continuation of either time or class. After a bit of back and forth, I agree I'll be ready for it ('Think of the money' is a great motivator) and drag myself out of bed to prep everything while eating breakfast. Not the biggest deal, except that adding the new prep and fielding the messages and creating the invoice eats my 'getting properly awake' time.

Class 1 (a company class) goes as well as usual. That is, Belle has lost her work, Kim hasn't done his, and Kim refuses to keep his camera on. Nothing new here.

Class 2 (a private class) is great. Lindsey and Amy are on good form and we take a virtual trip into London courtesy of the Oxford Reading Tree bunch and Google maps. I'd chatted to Amy's mum last night about whether Amy can write in English, and we agreed that she could cope with a few words in class but not too much more. She exceeds my expectations, and both girls write a few good sentences. They dictate more sentences, which I write onto the screen for them to copy. Amy stays focused throughout. Lindsey always stays focused; Amy is a year younger, and often doesn't.

So far so good. And then it's time for the 'sprung-upon-me' class. And here's how that goes:

Kayley (who I know from another class) has internet trouble. Mostly this means I can neither see nor hear her, although Zoom shows her as connected. She, apparently, can hear me fine. My interaction with Kayley consists of an endless loop of "Can you hear me?" "I don't know if you can hear me, but if you can..." and the odd brief interlude of "Oh there you are!" In the brief moments of clarity, she tries to answer anything I ask her classmates and I spend the rest of our communication reminding her to wait until I ask her directly. She doesn't really understand.

Sean, who I may have met once before, in a trial, but not necessarily the same trial – I can't remember; it was ages ago – is young, maybe only four or five. He arrives late, and loudly. I mute him before he even gets his camera on. He is attended only by his older sister, who I have also met before but who I don't recognise and whose name I have forgotten. She is about six years old. From background noise, of which there is plenty, I gather there may be grandparents in the room. Or perhaps an entire musical society in the living room. On their tea break. Talking loudly. At first, I think it might be a television, but Sean, who has great conversational skills and almost flawless English, despite his young age, says, "What's a television?" and that is as far as my suggestion to quieten his house goes. I mention this in feedback. Strongly.

Summer, who was scheduled to attend a trial class in November but didn't show up for it, pops up in class today but spends approximately forty minutes of the fifty minute lesson in the bathroom. With his camera off, which is great, as no one needs to witness forty minutes on the toilet, but also means I had no idea whether he is paying any level of attention, or is indeed even still on the toilet. He is also wearing a mask, which may be necessary coupled with his forty-minute toilet session, but adds to the difficulty in his communication skills.

Jerry, poor Jerry. Jerry arrives in class on time, sits focused and ram-rod upright throughout, tries his very best and dodges around a non-stop barrage of "Summer, are you still in the bathroom?", "Kayley, can you hear me?", and "Sean, I can't hear you." to give occasional correct answers or to read the odd sentence.

Classes like this are truly sent from hell. The only silver lining is that the company I currently work for is understanding, sympathetic, and offers me the right amount of head-patting, eye-rolling, and screaming emojis to let me know they are on my side. Feedback is often delayed on days like these, as I need to decompress in a quiet room first. Or at least make a cup of tea.

Thank goodness my afternoon students are two easy 30-minutes, first with Buse and then Mira, both from Turkiye, where we gossip as if we are besties, despite the nearly 40-year age gap between me and these 12 year olds.

However, I didn't predict needing to learn dentistry skills in order to reassure Buse that it is probably just one of her very last baby teeth that's wobbling at the back of her mouth after she ate a Haribo... The best thing about my chats with Buse is how we segue from teeth to gay rights to a fight with her mum to her Religion Studies teacher breaking the bin in class, without even taking a breath. These subjects flow into each other like water spilling across a desktop.

Monday January 9, 2023
Number of classes: 2
Number of students: 1+2
Lessons to plan for tomorrow: 1 (1/2, really, as I did most of it last night)

Poor Dorrie has exams again. I am certain that there are exams *at least* every other week in China and Taiwan.

Rain and Angelia seem to have forgotten almost everything. Again. They find the level of work hard enough without the two-week break we've just had. I'm glad I've no more classes today, and at least I got tomorrow's lesson plan finished in the gap between Dorrie's class and Rain and Angelia's. I think I need a break, even though I just had ten days off and only had three students today. Roll on Chinese New Year!

Tuesday January 10, 2023
Number of classes: 4
Number of students: 1+4+4+2
Lessons to plan for tomorrow: 1, because I did one of the 2 yesterday afternoon

Why, after two and a half years of reading Harry Potter, does Dorrie still read "wend" instead of "wand"? On the plus side, she has finally stopped calling him "Hurry".

One of the very most annoying things in this job, ever, is when a company throws a new student into a class without telling me. I have asked them over and over to not do this, and they are always apologetic and promise to do better. Rinse and repeat.

In today's first company class, Olivia shows up, about five minutes after the lesson begins.

Olivia is not in this class.

Olivia has tried a few different classes since her mum decided she was too good for the class she was initially a part of. Olivia has not been able for any of the other new classes she's tried so far, and would have been better off sticking with being the best in her class instead of the new girl who can't keep up with anything in any other mid-way-through-the-course class she's crashed into to try out. Olivia, nonetheless, is lovely, and an easy student, and to be fair, the class she joins today will suit her far better than any other she has tried to date. I just wish I'd known she was coming, so I don't have to interrupt the class to find out if she is supposed to be there.

Last year, I had a pair of private students (Sean and Harry) who were no longer well-matched, so I messaged Harry's mum to troubleshoot. Harry is one of my longest-term and most favourite students (if we had such things as favourites), so was my priority, and his mum agreed readily to heavily discounted one-to-one classes, when I explained that I wanted to split the two boys. His then-classmate Sean, I was willing to sacrifice. Aside from the mis-match of levels, Sean has a very pushy mother, and I hadn't the energy for her anymore. (He's not the same Sean as young-Sean from my company classes.) In a spate of genius, I contacted the parents of Harry's old classmate, Susie, and quickly and easily convinced her to re-join Harry for some literature classes, which I hope is going to work out fine. (We had their first *James and the Giant Peach* class last week, and so far so good.)

Sean, meanwhile, I had promised to try to find a solution for. I half-heartedly looked for a new classmate, after his mum was upset at the idea of me telling her I no longer had room for him. Then I took time off over Christmas and let it slide. Today, guilt kicks in, and I contact a couple of former colleagues to see if they have space for him. I spend a while this afternoon matchmaking and liaising with Sean's mum and the other teachers to try to set up a trial for Sean. I hope one of them works out for him, as I don't relish the idea of having to squeeze an extra lesson into my week at this final stage of my MA studies. Fingers crossed.

WEDNESDAY JANUARY 11, 2023
NUMBER OF CLASSES: 2
NUMBER OF STUDENTS: 3+2
LESSONS TO PLAN FOR TOMORROW: 1

I wake up to a message asking me to cover a couple of Romanian classes next week. These don't pay anything comparable to my morning classes, but they have proved to be fun and easy enough, and fit neatly into my afternoons, so I'll take the odd offer of cover classes when it suits me. I just need to remember to show up.

My first class this morning – my only company class today – is my favourite of the week. It's a literature class with three wonderful students. For the last two classes they've been joined by Bruno, but after I told his mother off last week, he has cancelled today's lesson. This may be a coincidence – I've known Bruno for a while as he was a student of mine in my previous company too. We only recently rediscovered each other in the summer when I covered a class after another teacher left. However, I won't tolerate parents yelling at their children in my class, or disrupting, so my feedback was strongly worded after the last class. So with Bruno absent, Honey, Sophia, and Natalie were back to their well-established threesome. The book we finished today was fun, and sad as it sounds, I may even reread it just for fun. Who cares if it's middle-grade? Not me anyway.

Wednesdays are easy.

Thursday January 12th, 2023
Number of classes: 3
Number of students: 3+3-ish+3
Lessons to plan for tomorrow: 1

Today I have a new experience. Nimo (aka Craig) takes the first part of his class from the back of a bike. At least, I hope it's the back, and he's not simultaneously steering the bike through a busy Chinese city full of highrise buildings while taking his weekly English class. Brightly-lit highrise buildings are silhouetted against a darkening sky. It's all very picturesque. I presume, at first, he is walking, and ask him to stop for a moment and show me around. This is the moment I discover he is on a bike.

The topic of this lesson is 'Spring'. This causes a new discussion, as the biking student lives far enough south that he doesn't experience spring in the same way as the lesson materials present it. His seasons pretty much blend together into one long, warm summer. He tells me today was 16 degrees Celsius. Google tells me it averaged at 18°C in his city today, with highs of 21°C. The main thing we learn from this is that I want to live there too.

Alice, meanwhile, begins class from the backseat of a car, flanked by two friends, one of whom I know from other classes. By the time they get home, the other two have already lost interest in the class and are chatting amongst themselves, softly, but just loudly enough to be distracting.

Later, in class three, we have an unusual approach to problem and solution:

PROBLEM: I have too much homework.
SOLUTION: The dog can eat the homework.
PROBLEM: The dog has eaten the homework.
SOLUTION: Eat the dog.
PROBLEM: I have eaten the dog.
And then:
PROBLEM: Mum says, "Where is the dog?"
SOLUTION: I can buy a new dog.

Luffy, Cynthia, and Vincent are developing excellent collaborative story-telling skills.

Friday January 13th, 2023
Number of classes: 5
Number of students: 2+2+2+1+1
Lessons to plan for Monday: 0

Well, this is significantly more pleasant that last Friday. The chaos class that was thrown on me last week is, today, calm, quiet, and perfectly pleasant thanks to the absence of internet issues, bathroom visits, grandparents, and two of the four students. It is also greatly enhanced by the supervising presence of Sean's mum and the fact I expected the class today and am prepared for it to be far worse than it is.

It's the time of year when students are on their long winter holiday and either take classes on the move, from hotels, or cancel them completely. The highs and the lows, all bundled together.

This afternoon, Buse continues to put her skill in Olde-English insults to good use, telling me that she has broken up with her crusty-arsed wazzock of a boyfriend.

MONDAY JANUARY 16TH, 2023
NUMBER OF CLASSES: 3
NUMBER OF STUDENTS: 1+3+4
LESSONS TO PLAN FOR TOMORROW: 1

Xika is joining Rain and Angelia's class for the rest of the course popped into my messages over the weekend. No problem. I met Xika once before; she has better English than either Rain or Angelia, but that's no bad thing.

When I enter the classroom this morning, there are no students waiting. This is unusual, but they still have time; I'm a few minutes early.

Rain arrives.

Kind of.

In that his name comes up, and the black Zoom square of a hiding participant. He doesn't turn on his camera or mic. Again, not unusual – often the parent gets the classroom ready and then yells at the student to come and join once I turn on my own camera. Rain, and Angelia, however, are usually here and ready to chat. I ask a few times if he is there but he doesn't reply. I wait.

At exactly the time we should start the class, I send a message. The response is swift:

Angelia has asked for leave.
I will call Rain and Xika, Fiona[4] adds, a moment later.

After about five minutes, Rain turns on his camera. He hasn't good enough English to explain where he was or what he'd been doing. It's good for him to have some one-to-one time, and we settle in to discuss today's lesson topic of how he can help his community.

He remembers, with much amusement and pride, that we can plant plants (as prompted by a picture, but the words entirely his own). So far so good. And then he tells me he can help in his neighbourhood by planting turtles.

Me: "Turtles? Are you sure?"

Rain: "Yes."

I draw the scenario on the screen.

After some time, and many drawings of turtle-plants, Rain realises he means tomatoes. Ah. Yes, growing tomatoes could indeed be more beneficial to the community. Out of all my students, Rain (perhaps by virtue of being one of the lowest-level students) makes the most of this kind of mistakes. We have a running class joke about his frequent puppy/people/poppy confusion.

---

4. Fiona is one of my Chinese colleagues/class co-ordinators, and it is she who deals with most of my problems, and works with me to find solutions. I have never met Fiona, but I adore her.

Xika's mum has arrived home by now. It turns out Xika has been alone with her grandparents, trying to join class, but with no combined knowledge as to how to turn on the camera or mic in the Zoom platform. Most of my students' grandparents are younger than me, so it seems strange that even now, after the whole pandemic/lockdown/everyone-using-Zoom thing of the last few years, so many of the grandparents still don't know how to use it.

The biggest surprise of the class is yet to come. Ten minutes before the end of class, Angelia shows up. Not on leave after all, then.

In my evening class – one of the Romanian classes I'm covering this week – one student has an absolutely perfect English Boarding School accent. She talks about her goals for the year ahead and her horses as if she is speaking to the queen. Another student tells me he is learning English and Spanish so he can speak to everyone in the world.

I ask him if he is planning to speak to everyone in the world.

Tuesday January 17th, 2023
Number of classes: 6
Number of students: 1+4+4+2+2+4
Lessons to plan for tomorrow: 1

I only finished the fourth class ten minutes ago and I already can't remember anything specific about any of this morning's classes. I feel as if I've talked a lot today, and my throat is aching. Catherine and Mango are trudging through *Wonder*, and although Mango says she is enjoying it and finding it okay to read, she is finding it hard to answer any comprehension-check questions.

I've left them thinking about this dilemma: Is it better to ask August about his face, or to pretend there is nothing unusual about his face and not mention it at all? Mango thinks it's okay to ask; Catherine thinks it's not. I wonder if they will have changed their minds when I see them next.

In the first of my two Romanian cover classes, I spend 45 minutes colouring with two lovely girls. Can't complain. (In my defence, we did a lot of talking, predicting, guessing, and general chat while we were at it. Then we spent the last ten minutes cramming in a bunch of 'real-seeming work' too.) In the second class, we spend an extra seventeen minutes after the class should have finished trying to guess four Hangman games at once.

Today is the day I learn that doing four simultaneous games of Hangman is a little optimistic. Luckily I have nowhere better to be.

WEDNESDAY JANUARY 18TH, 2023
NUMBER OF CLASSES: 5
NUMBER OF STUDENTS: 1+2+2+1+1
LESSONS TO PLAN FOR TOMORROW: 1

Today begins with every online teacher's nightmare – my computer has a meltdown. Still trying to help ex-student Sean find a new teacher, I am trying to send some files to another teacher. My laptop has been running a bit slow this week, and the fan is running loudly. The things I am trying to do are not, well, *doing*, so I begin to close things down so I can restart. And then the screen goes black.

Luckily, after a frantic phone call to my husband and a brief panic, I manage to fix it. Luckily, also, the student I am supposed to be meeting on the conversational platform is one I have a Facebook contact with. Usually, companies aren't happy for teachers to have direct communication with students – poaching clients to give private lessons is a **big bad thing** in this game, but I only have four, very long-term

(4+ years, mostly) students who I still meet on this particular platform – it simply doesn't pay enough to give any more hours to, and as I've had these students so long, I've managed to get contact details for them all. I message the student to explain, and manage to log on only seven minutes late, with no impact on any other classes. Phew.

Thursday January 19th, 2023
Number of classes: 3
Number of students: 2+3+2
Lessons to plan for tomorrow: 1

The day begins with one of my favourite lessons in the course: We have to create a monster and write a short story about it. Only Luna and Evelyn are in class, and they begin by sharing the stories they wrote last week, in which they chose to make me the main character. The setting they chose is America, and my problem, eerily accurate to my real life, is that I am having trouble finding food I like. In Evelyn's story, I ask the chef to cook me some eggs, and I wonder if Evelyn has been that fly on the wall in any of a zillion restaurants I have eaten in. It's hard work being a vegetarian coeliac, but Evelyn didn't know this about me when she wrote her story.

Both girls' stories ended with me going home, hungry and unsatisfied. Art imitating life.

Now, on to the monster. We spend five minutes drawing a monster. I'm quite pleased with mine, although my attempt from the last time I taught this class may've been better. Today's effort is a blue, three-eyed, sad, furry creature. Next, we write a quick profile, and my sad furry monster realises he loves to play chess but is no good at it. When we brainstorm the problem our monster may face, mine comes easily – he needs to learn how to play chess, but his mentor lives somewhere hot (not under the cold rock my dude inhabits, but out in the open blazing heat of *Somewhere*).

I'm not the one who needs to write a story though, and I haven't the energy today to work out where this could go, so I abandon my furry blue monster and make the odd encouraging comment to the girls. They, meanwhile, are scribbling away, punctuating the silence with odd requests for spellings. I like this part – the words they ask for give me clues as to where their stories are heading: *Kill. Person. Before. Try. Excited.* I already know that Evelyn's pencil-case-dwelling little one-eyed creature is going to turn nasty. I'm surprised he's able, what with moving like a rotten pear, sliding along on his legless body. Luna's monster is the excited one, but overall, she asks for help with fewer words, so it's hard to predict her story.

In the second class, Kevin, Craig, and Alice are writing instructions about how to care for pets.

Alice: *The sheep is a dangerous pet.*

Kevin: *Triceratops meat is best. Take it for a walk four times each day in the jungle.*

Craig: *You need to buy three king cobras a day. You can use badger spray to defeat it.*

The main thing I learn in this class is that I will look after Alice's imaginary pet sheep but not Craig's badger or Kevin's T-Rex.

In the last class, the *silly* keeps on coming. This last Thursday class is hilarious every week, and this one does not disappoint. It's Chinese New Year next week, and apparently Cynthia's older brother is actually a rabbit, who will eat Luffy, but Luffy has already eaten all his homework and Cynthia has eaten her teacher — me, I suspect — so I'm not sure anyone will be going hungry around here.

Luffy's sentence of wisdom today fulfils his brief to use the word 'word' in a sentence: "I have a funny word: laugh."

He's not wrong. It makes me laugh a lot.

Favourites among Cynthia's sentences are: "I don't like soggy worms." and "Some girls are stupid."

I don't like worms either, but I don't just reject the soggy ones.

Friday January 20th, 2023
Number of classes: 5
Number of students: 3+2+3+1+1
Lessons to plan for tomorrow: 0

It's a refreshing change when there isn't much to say.

Yesterday's 'Lessons to Plan: 1' went a bit awry when I realised late in the day that I had to create TWO entire lessons from scratch, not just one, and I was already half-asleep and wondering if I could get away with doing the one I thought I needed to do in the morning instead. I decided not, and got on with it. They didn't take too long, and *Victorian Adventure*[5], *Day 1*, was created with a background of The Apprentice keeping me company. But I was late to bed, and tired, so I'm grateful for the easy classes of the morning.

In the afternoon, things get more interesting.

In my first conversation class, Buse informs me, in rapid English that her loitering Grandmother won't be able to understand, that as part of a 'new trend' she deliberately set fire to her own finger. She's my most intelligent student. She

---

5. Hunt, R, and Brychta, A, *Victorian Adventure*, Oxford University Press, 1990

speaks four or five languages. She's smart. But not as smart as I had been fooled into believing. She shows me her finger.

I have no lessons next week. Most of my students are on Winter break, and Chinese New Year begins this weekend. When my Chinese students have holidays, I usually cancel my other classes too. I'm cashing in on their holiday to take my own.

Monday January 30th, 2023
Number of classes: 2
Number of students: 1+3
Lessons to plan for tomorrow: 1

I've had the most blissful week away at a writing retreat in Gladstone's Library[6] and I haven't missed working at all. There was one uncomfortable moment when I extracted myself from the bowels of a silent reading room at about 11.30 on the Friday morning for a quick breather and found a message from Amy's mum wondering whether we had class. Seems that although I'd told the girls in class on the last Friday,

---

6. The UK's only residential library and a truly blissful place for a writing retreat. https://www.gladstoneslibrary.org/

I forgot to tell the parents, and the girls had arrived into our Zoom room at 11 A.M. as usual. Oops.

Work really started again yesterday, with messages trickling in about 'Can I fit in a new class?' and suchlike, but as Monday is an easy day with no prep needed, I managed to mostly ignore it.

It would be lying to say I'm now back in the thick of it, as I only have 30 minutes with Dorrie at 9 A.M. chatting about life and reading Harry Potter, and then a 55-minute class at 11.10 A.M. And that's it. This week anyway. I've offered 10 A.M. as the possible slot for the new class, so I imagine that could start next week.

It is my intention to plan tomorrow AND Wednesday's literature lessons this afternoon, but as it is also my intention to make something fabulous for dinner, work on my MA, walk the dogs and maybe even spend some time in the garden, I already know that I will not get all three literature lessons made today.

Tuesday January 31st, 2023
Number of classes: 4
Number of students: 1+3+4+2
Lessons to plan for tomorrow: 1

I did manage to do two full lesson plans on Monday, luckily taking pressure off today. I was up until 1 A.M., due to a neighbour crisis, so today was a bleary-eyed, yawny, auto-pilot kind of day, and I am still scoffing muesli when Dorrie calls at 9am.

My 10 A.M. class is easy, too.

The 11 A.M. class comes and goes with a little more effort – the students in my 11 A.M. Tuesday class are my lowest-level students. Today's lesson is supposed to involve creating their own story. These students still struggle with CHARACTER and SETTING, and even 'Who?' and 'Where?' (particularly 'Where?'). Apple, bless her, can't even understand that this is a STORY we're trying to create, and we got as far as *A girl called Apple was jumping rope.*

"I'm not jumping rope," she says.

I remind her it's a story, and pretend, and we move on to the *where* her story needs. One of her classmates helps out and we limp along to "Apple was jumping rope in the playground." After another painful round of non-responses, I throw in the PROBLEM element:

"A dog comes along and wants to play too," I suggest.

Apple is most indignant: "I don't have a dog."

Me: "It's a *story*."

And round and round we go.

Meanwhile, Kayley's story sounds suspiciously like a retelling of what happened to her for real earlier today (she has swimming lessons on a Tuesday before coming to this class) but does at least contain a character (her dad), a setting (swimming pool), and a problem, bringing with it a new character: **Kayley** doesn't like swimming.

Eric, in true Eric fashion, is the one to drag some imagination to the party and we finally get something resembling the lesson goal: Eric (because imagination only goes so far) was at a volcano. It was dangerous so he wanted to go home. He made a boat and went home. Then it was all a dream.

Bobby Ewing, eat your heart out. Scriptwriters, stand aside. Directors, get ready; a blockbuster is on the way.

January, thank goodness, is over.

February

Wednesday February 1st, 2023
Number of classes: 5
Number of students: 1+4+2+1+1
Lessons to plan for tomorrow: 1

Today started easily and gently at 10 a.m., with Richard and I watching a Mr Beast video. It also means we know what we will talk about next week – I'm not convinced the video (*50 hours in Antarctica*) was really filmed in Antarctica, so next week we'll do some research and try to find out if it was faked. I can already see the headlines: ESL teacher and 12-year-old student expose greatest You-Tuber of our time during 30-min conversation lesson. This could be the thing that makes me rich. Or gets me killed.

The other two Wednesday classes are always equally enjoyable. The first is a literature-based class with three amazing girls who have an understanding of life equal to any coffee morning with three old women! In the text we are studying this week there is a nasty child called Cynthia. All three classmates shared stories of a real-life Cynthia they know. Honey has spoken before about being bullied in school, and it's times like these that I wish I could reach through the webcam and meet these students for real. Honey spent her Chinese New Year week making a box-bed for a stray street-dog.

In my last class, Harry and Susie have recently reunited after about eighteen months apart – I haven't seen Susie in that interim but Harry has been a consistent student for years now and stayed with me as a private student after the collapse of ESL Companies across China in summer 2021. Harry's new classmate (Sean) wasn't at the same level as Harry, and I could see Harry was becoming bored in class, so at the start of December I told both students' parents that this partnership wasn't working any more.

I was prepared to give Harry one-to-one and suggested a literature-based class for him too, based partly on the fun I have in the earlier Wednesday class. We agreed easily on *James and the Giant Peach* and then in a moment of optimism I texted Susie's mum to see if Susie wanted to join us.

And she did.

So I have my favourite pairing together again. In the first couple of classes, Harry was a little quieter, and I wasn't yet convinced that putting them together again would work. Susie, chatterbox still, had no such reluctance. However, today felt like they have settled in and Harry was chatty and the two picked up their old style of disagreeing with each other and taking opposing sides to many of the things discussed. I'm delighted. My greatest achievement in my time in Whales English[1] was teaching this pair to argue, and it's truly a great thing to hear! My-old-married-couple pair is well-and-truly back.

I send Harry's mum a message after class.

Me: *I think Harry seems happier in the classes now. Is he enjoying them better.*

Her: *Maybe.*

Later in the day, Buse and I debate the power of God, should he/she/it exist.

Thursday February 2nd 2023
Number of classes: 3
Number of students: 1+3+2
Lessons to plan for tomorrow: 1

Lots of the students are still on holiday this week and many of today's are missing, late, or taking class in a location that is not their home.

The first class brings a mixed blessing: some lovely and useful one-to-one with Luna, where we discuss info-dumps and I try to encourage her to weave her character description into her story instead of listing it all at the start, but as the lesson is supposed to introduce a new 6-week topic and her classmates are absent, I already know that next week will be chaotic while I instruct two students about something their third member is already wanting to begin.

In the second class, Alice is in a restaurant, which is lovely, and shows me the food they are eating. It is also not lovely, as she has no pen or paper, and gets up to leave the restaurant and travel home about ten minutes into the class. On the plus side, it's not as noisy as restaurants in China sometimes are.

Craig arrives late, still wearing his BMX helmet. He too, is not fully present in the class, and takes most of it from the back seat of a friend's car. He also has no pen or paper. This class is a writing class, so the lesson doesn't go so well.

The third class contains the delight that is Luffy and Cynthia. We're talking about how to build a ship, and it's a bit above-level for them, but they manage to make it fun, largely by drawing sinking ships and then telling me the entire book was about spaceships. My Thursdays were tiresome and hard work for a while, but some tiny shifts in student groupings means now they are really quite bearable, most weeks. Even from restaurants and BMX parks.

Friday February 3rd 2023
Number of classes: 5
Number of students: 1+3+3+1+1
Lessons to plan for Monday: 1

I have a new course on Monday, that has been newly-designed as a bridging class for some of my lower-level students, at my suggestion. It looks pretty good and won't need much tweaking before I teach it, so the prep won't take too long.

In my first class, Kim is unusually attentive. He even keeps his camera on for about ten minutes of the class, although the minutes are far from consecutive. It's a better class than it usually is, since it's only him and Belle today and not any of the recent flurry of trial students who have appeared in this course, so we can at least get on with discussing the ongoing project we have supposed to have been working on for the last 6 weeks. Mostly, we have done none of this, as the trial students have no idea what we've been doing and have no work for a project. Most weeks, nor has Kim. This week was no different in that respect – he still didn't bring his work to class.

I get a message mid-class to ask if I will teach another literature class. This course is well-planned and fun, although I can't really spare the time. The thought of it helping pay for my holiday tips the balance, and it's a quick yes.

In today's private class, Amy's mum is not home yet, so we have the usual rigmarole of no one else in her family knowing how to successfully make Zoom work. I can see her, and watch her dad or grandfather poking fruitlessly at the screen for the first few minutes. I text her mum, who fixes it from afar.

Sean and Jerry, in the third class, are low level. Sean is a cutie – only about 5 years old, and I think my youngest student. His spoken English is good, and he can be quite chatty. I'm impressed at his reasons for thinking a pig is not a good pet, as the book focuses on 'too big'. Sean offers a less body-shaming alternative: 'too stinky'. Jerry just yawns, mostly. Yawning students is probably the most difficult thing to deal with, even including tech issues, rowdy students, loud backgrounds, walking along streets, or bouncing along in cars. Yawning students starts me yawning, and then all is lost.

Buse, later in the afternoon, begins the chat with flashing her mum's credit card at the screen, telling me she stole it earlier today. She then proceeds to turn her tongue blue by eating what Google tells us are sweets with the acidity of battery acid. Our lesson ends abruptly because neither of us are paying attention to the time. I send a message.

Me: *I'm so glad we got cut off.*
Buse: *lmao*

Monday February 6th 2023
Number of classes: 3
Number of students: 1+2+3
Lessons to plan for tomorrow: 0

It's my birthday today. I'm 50 before the day is out, and in terms of online ESL this is quite old. I'm lucky to have a great clientele that appreciates age over blonde youth, but it's amazing how many of the old ESL companies preferred stereotypically blonde-haired, white-skinned 20-somethings over capability to teach or speak English. The company I work for now, and the last company I worked for before the ESL

China crash a couple of years ago have a better insight than most and value teachers with years of experience.

Not only is it my birthday, but it's also a brand new bank holiday in Ireland. It was first introduced last year, and I thought it was just a one-off to apologise for all the missed holidays during Covid, but turns out it's for St Brigid's Day and will come around on the first Monday in February every year.

As I had no idea, I agreed to start a new class today.

Luckily, it was easy to prep, easy to teach, and has passed without effort. The only downside is that for some reason both my company classes on a Monday now have weird start/finish times so I now have a fifteen-minute break after Dorrie, then a 30-minute break between the next two, which is somewhat disjointed and not quite long enough to be useful.

The last lesson of the morning is one of my least favourite. It's another of the over-American texts, and also way above level for the three students in this class. I don't even know the difference between sopranos, altos, bass and tenor, so I certainly don't expect them too, even if they did have the English skills needed to explain it.

Tuesday February 7th 2023
Number of classes: 3
Number of students: 1+3+4
Lessons to plan for tomorrow: 3

I thought I only had two classes to prepare, as tomorrow's new class is one I've taught before. I get a message at about lunchtime to tell me there's been a meeting and we are dividing the story books for that class over two weeks. This is both excellent news, as it's something I've suggested before, and bad news, as it now means I have an extra class to prep. I decide this will be the quickest one to prepare and I will do it first. I'm still feeling ill – sore throat, headache, etc – so I message back to say we'll wing it a bit but I'll check where to cut the lesson and where I can add writing exercises, then I get to work. I have just finished when they message me to say they have prepped it for me, to save me some time.

The third class I prep is the next *James and the Giant Peach*. We will cover the chapter where the peach tumbles off the White Cliffs of Dover, and I am remarkably calmed by listening to Vera Lynn singing about bluebirds as I add that song to the lesson. I haven't had time to do the other bazillion things on my list, like get on with my MA or call my mother, but now I'm finished, I'm done for the day and will head to bed with Nurofen. Or the sofa with wine.

Wednesday February 8th 2023
Number of classes: 5
Number of students: 1+4+3+1+1
Lessons to plan for tomorrow: 1

One Literature course begins as another ends. In the new one, Boson, a student I've never met before, shows up late. And loud. He comes in with his mother talking in the background. He interrupts to tell me he's here (fair enough) and then to offer a lengthy explanation about why he's late. He then answers over other students, loses connection, re-enters, loudly, again, and continues to talk over everyone else. His English is good; he knows the work, but if he's planning on joining this course, he'd better bring some classroom manners along.

On Monday, a massive earthquake decimated much of Turkiye and Syria. I somehow missed the news until talking to a Turkish friend last night. This evening, both Mira and Buse (both safe and relatively far away from the carnage) tell me of people they know or know of who have been killed or otherwise affected. Buse has a particularly horrific tale of her cousins' grandmother, who died from impact, and her sister's friend who died of the cold while awaiting rescue. At times like this, I feel very helpless. Buse, however, swiftly moves on, and tells me about her new puppy, who is peeing everywhere. The circle of life, I guess.

Thursday February 9th 2023
Number of classes: 3
Number of students: 3+2+4
Lessons to plan for tomorrow: 1

I wake at about 8 a.m. to find a message about a trial student joining one of the day's classes. I fire off a quick response – this is short notice, this is not a lesson for a trial student, we are in the middle of an ongoing project, I don't have time to change the lesson, etc. We've had this discussion before. By 9 a.m. I am at my computer and realise the trial wasn't for the class I thought. Not so bad. To be quite fair, he was a lovely student and fitted his lesson well. Lucky escape. Meanwhile the lesson I thought he was joining would have been okay either, since the only student who showed up last week was 30 minutes late, and the other two have to start the project from scratch anyway. Ah well.

FRIDAY FEBRUARY 10TH 2023
NUMBER OF CLASSES: 5
NUMBER OF STUDENTS: 2+2+1+1+1
LESSONS TO PLAN FOR MONDAY: 1

My feedback for Kim was not complimentary. He is, frankly a pain in the butt. He rarely puts his camera on, despite endless requests, and he doesn't respond to questions. This is not because he can't – he has great spoken English. I have no idea if he is paying attention or doing any work, and I don't know why he comes to class.

In Lindsey and Amy's private class, we are still talking about Victorian Britain. In our book, Biff, Chip, and Kipper get sent to jail.[2] This led us to question whether children really did go to jail in Victorian times. This led us to discover that children as young as eight were not only sent to prison, but also hanged. If this wasn't a gruesome enough sidetrack, Kipper became worried that he may get his head chopped off. Luckily, we already knew this was more of a Henry VIII kind of thing, so

---

2. Hunt, R, and Brychta, A, *Victorian Adventure*, Oxford Reading Tree, 1990

we could skim on past this a bit quicker. Amy didn't cry, but I won't be surprised if she has nightmares. Sorry Amy.

Monday February 13th 2023
Number of classes: 3
Number of students: 1+2+3
Lessons to plan for tomorrow: 1

I wake up to find messages 'asking' if I am okay with having five students in two of my company classes. These classes are usually a maximum of four, and more often only two or three students. Of course, more is better for the company, financially, and I get no extra (or less) pay if the numbers change, but in terms of delivering a good class that the students gain full benefit from, having extra students can be detrimental. In both the classes they are suggesting adding more students to, the students are lower level and need all the talk-time they can get. In both classes I have a student who needs a lot of time to formulate any spoken English, and with extra students they simply won't have the luxury of this thinking time. These students will be severely compromised by adding more children. One child has already proven that she performs far better in a smaller class but clams up in a larger one, so I doubt she'll speak at all in a group of five! Plus, more feedback to write each week too. I present my opinion (bar the grumble about feedback, as in other classes I only have two children, so this does even out) and suggest that maybe the company is growing well enough to take on another teacher.

"Yes," they agree, "but these students want you." And that's a hard point to argue with!

Tuesday February 14th 2023
Number of classes: 4
Number of students: 1+3+4+2
Lessons to plan for tomorrow: 0

I must take a moment to feel smug, as the Lessons to Plan for Tomorrow would have read '3' but I did them all yesterday. Phew.

Today starts with the thing online teachers dread – a lack of sufficient internet speeds to connect to my first class. My computer has been running noisily for the last week or so, and eventually I restart it, rather than rebooting the router yet again. This seems to fix the issue, whatever it was, and the rest of the day's classes pass without hitch. Internet-wise, at least.

In my first company class, I get a message to say Angelia will be late, due to her own internet issues. This is a surprise in that I thought Angelia had dropped out of this class anyway – we haven't seen her on a Tuesday for weeks.

In the second company class, we read a simple book about France. I have supplemented the book by adding maps – world, Europe, and then just France. I show the students on each map where France is, and discuss that it is a country far from China but close to where I live. Then we read the book, look at the pictures, Google-map our way across Paris, get a street view of the Eiffel Tower and Arc de Triomph, and so on. Tasked with writing about France, I write the header 'France' and give the students keywords from the book. I ask them to tell me what they have just learned about France.

Apple asks, "Teacher, what is France?"

Wednesday February 15th 2023
Number of classes: 5
Number of students: 2+3+2+1+1
Lessons to plan for tomorrow: 1

Even with having added a new class last week, Wednesdays are still the best day each week – three literature-based classes, all with reasonably easy students and two with fantastic students.

Harry and Susie have settled back into their old stride as if they hadn't been separated for over a year, and we are having a lot of fun with *James and the Giant Peach*. Their homework today is to choose the most disgusting food listed in the Centipede's Chapter 18 song, and then to begin next week by persuading each other how delicious each one's chosen food is. Yum.

Sophia, Honey, and Natalie, meanwhile, begin their new level today and come to class with a collection of great questions they've thought up based on having read the first three chapters. Sophia, today, is reading like a writer, and offers comments about why the author made certain choices with the storyline. Honey explains to us all that if a stray cat has been thrown out of its home, it is likely to be more friendly, but if a cat is born a stray, it will be unfriendly. She is very observant about stray animals, and only last week told us about her feeding a street dog. This is a truly inspiring and inspirational class and these girls are a bright hope for the future.

I am contacted today by an previous student's father, asking if I can take on some new students looking for beginner lessons. I don't really have time, but I will try to squeeze them in – I haven't had any real beginners for ages.

Thursday February 16th 2023
Number of classes: 3
Number of students: 3+3+4
Lessons to plan for tomorrow: 1 (half, really, as I did most of it last night)

Funny how Thursdays changed from being manic and headache-inducing to being calm and fun so fast. It's only a couple of months since I lost it completely after three hellish Thursday classes on the bounce and drew up a very firmly-worded reminder of class expectations to be sent to all the students. Since then, possibly helped by small changes in students attending the classes too, the classes have become not only bearable again, but a lovely mix of easy, calm, and hilariously fun. The highlight of today – or possibly the low point – is Kevin interrupting the class to inform us that he is about to go to the toilet and could be gone for a long time. Far more information than we need.

The potential new students' mother from yesterday tries some back-and-forth WeChat-messaged negotiations on price. I tell her I've already reduced my prices, since the class is for siblings, and that she can take some time to think it over – I'm in no rush and won't offer the time to anyone else. She immediately replies accepting my terms. How easy it is to stand ground, sometimes.

FRIDAY FEBRUARY 17TH 2023
NUMBER OF CLASSES: 5
NUMBER OF STUDENTS: 2+2+4+1+1
LESSONS TO PLAN FOR MONDAY: 1

My ranty feedback to Kim last week has had some effect. He put his camera on for about three seconds, only, but did at least appear to pay good attention and work well.

Buse is bonding well with her new puppy and seems to be more accepting that it is a baby and will need to learn stuff before it knows stuff. It's so cute, and our entire lesson is basically her showing me the dog and me saying, "He's so cute."

Monday February 20th 2023
Number of classes: 2
Number of students: 1+2
Lessons to plan for tomorrow: 1

Today's trial class has been bumped to next week, which I am pleased about, as I wake to the news that my grandfather died last night.

Sky and Apple have fun in our meerkat-themed class, despite a repeated consensus that the meerkats are all very ugly. I am impressed at how chatty and excited they are by this class, and it bodes well for this new partnership.

Tuesday February 21st 2023
Number of classes: 4
Number of students: 1+3+4+2
Lessons to plan for tomorrow: 2 (because I did one yesterday evening)

Having only been reminded last Tuesday that Angelia does in fact still attend the first of today's two company classes, she didn't turn up again today. I guess she's far too busy training to become China's next Olympic Figure Skater. I've seen videos;

I'm not joking. Angelia doesn't go to school – she trains almost every day. She's seven or eight years old. She's also not my only figure-skater student.

Honey, as ever, is brimming with amazing ideas for her stories, but she simply can't manage to actually WRITE the ideas down. Today's idea is so good that I may have to steal it and use it for myself. I think she just doesn't have the confidence to allow her ideas to spill out randomly, so I do hope she moves on from that. Here is the scenario she has thought up:

> A normal person is living a normal life amongst normal people. He wakes up under the sofa, where he always sleeps, in his pink dress, which he sleeps in. He writes on the bed – and she doesn't mean he sits on the bed, propped against comfy pillows. She means he uses the bed as paper. He thinks he's normal, but really, he's not that normal after all, and his whole story is unfolding when we talk about him, but she can't write any of it down. So it will be forgotten.
>
> Honey

In my second company class, Apple is still on a high from yesterday's ugly meerkats, and as our text today is about beavers, it's easy to continue the *ugly* theme. I'm not entirely sure I should be encouraging this judgement based on animals' looks, but it's just so funny and all four students are in fits of laughter as they describe each animal as ugly. Sometimes you've just got to let political correctness standards slip to enjoy the students use of English and to let them have fun with it. To be fair, the crocodile Kayley draws IS a bit ugly. It has feet (I presume) that look like udders. Dangerous? You'd die laughing.

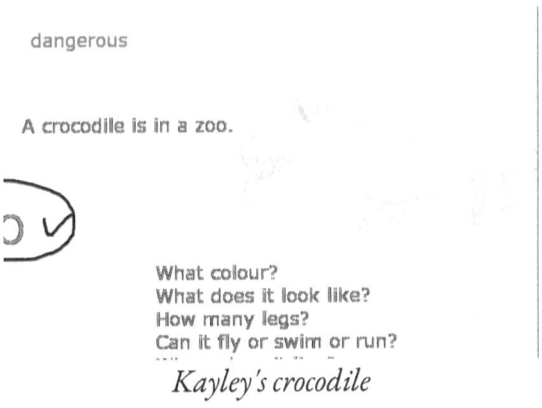

Kayley's crocodile

My last class today drags into a long internet-or-device issue for Catherine, so we don't get so far through the lesson as I'd planned for. This is the true beauty of private lessons – **It doesn't matter.** We can just pick up from wherever we got to next time.

WEDNESDAY FEBRUARY 22ND 2023
NUMBER OF CLASSES: 6
NUMBER OF STUDENTS: 3+3+2+1+1+
LESSONS TO PLAN FOR TOMORROW: 1

In the second of my literature classes, the girls spend so long talking about everything under the sun that we barely have time to talk about the four chapters of *My Father's Dragon*[3] they are supposed to have read. Honey has only managed one chapter anyway, and Natalie two or three of the four, but the joy of working with this company is that I simply send a message to say we will extend this book by an extra week.

Harry and Susie have a fabulous argument to try to convince each other that mice with rice is nice (Susie convincing Harry), or that mosquito toes and wampfish roes are nice (Harry convincing Susie). Their arguments are smooth and well-thought out, and to be honest, I am *almost* tempted by the mosquito toes, once they are fried to a crisp. They are, after all, very small. However, no amount of convincing would persuade me on mice with rice.

---

3. Gannett, Ruth Stiles, *My Father's Dragon*, 1948, Random House

Buse forgets to come to her class until about ten minutes before her time is up. I'd rather a full no-show, which I'd have got the ten minutes pay for anyway!

Thursday February 23rd 2023
Number of classes: 3
Number of students: 2+3+4
Lessons to plan for tomorrow: 0 (Amy and Lindsey have cancelled)

If I am organised, I will plan Lindsey and Amy's class anyway. It will put me ahead for next week.

Luna, once again, does a large part of her class alone. Evelyn is there throughout, but eating her dinner with her camera off. Teresa, as usual, is late. She is also eating. Today's warm-up write is about favourite sports or activities. Luna's favourite sport is basketball, so I ask her why. It's because if she had a dog, it would like to watch basketball. To clarify: Luna likes basketball, which she doesn't actually play, because the dog she doesn't actually have might like to watch her play.

Friday February 24th 2023
Number of classes: 4
Number of students: 2+3+1+1
Lessons to plan for Monday: 1

I have great intentions to plan Monday's lesson in the gap where Lindsey and Amy's class should be, but my company has not yet uploaded the outline to our shared drive, so that is the end of that good idea.

I don't let the gift of a spare hour go entirely to waste, and after making a cuppa, check some quotes I'm referencing in my MA project.

Kim and Belle's class is remarkably pleasant and easy today, with both students coming to class well-prepared with lots of storyline to discuss. This summarising of their work-in-progress is followed by ten minutes of independent writing, and then a 15-minute video, so I carry on with my own work quietly in the background too. Nice.

MONDAY FEBRUARY 27TH 2023
NUMBER OF CLASSES: 3
NUMBER OF STUDENTS: 1+2+3
LESSONS TO PLAN FOR TOMORROW: 0 (BECAUSE I JUST FINISHED THE ONE I NEEDED TO DO BEFORE WRITING THIS.)

Apple has no imagination beyond telling me that squirrels and other cute animals are ugly. I have noticed this before, but here is today's example:

For pre-learning vocabulary needed in the lesson, I show Apple and Sky a picture of some garden tools, labelled. Gloves, rake, trowel, shovel or spade. The image is headed 'Garden tools'. I ask the students what these tools are for. No answer, so I give them a choice.

Me: "Would you use these tools in the garden or to cook your dinner?"

Apple: "I don't have a garden."

Me: "If you did have a garden, would you use these tool in the garden or to cook your dinner?"

Apple: "I don't cook dinner."

Me: "But if you did..."

Apple: "I don't have a garden or help cook dinner."

Followed not long after by, "Squirrels are ugly."

Some you win, some you lose. But aside from ugly animals and a lack of imagination this class is going remarkably well and is very enjoyable. Sky and Apple are chatting A LOT and asking A LOT of questions (like **all the time**) and making great progress, which is more than can be said for the next class, where not one student has prepared for the class by reading the story, or by bringing suitable writing materials to class.

Tuesday February 28th 2023
Number of classes: 4
Number of students: 1+4+4+2
Lessons to plan for tomorrow: 3

Today's bizarre twist is that Apple thinks Kayley's silkworms are cute. This is the same Apple who announced that meerkats (adults and babies), rabbits, beavers, squirrels, and every other animals we have seen in the last two weeks is ugly. But the tiny wriggly caterpillar/worm things Kayley held on her hand, they are cute.

In today's literature class, Honey introduces us to the wonders of text-to-speech and how well/badly it coped with her narration.

Some problems with it are merely down to punctuation is the wrong places, or repetition where Honey was thinking allowed. Other parts are more confusing and gave us a lot of fun in trying to decode the story. Pizza, apparently, is peeking. My favourite line is 'The supermarket doesn't let pants.' Pets, if you are wondering. I don't think AI is quite ready for taking over the world of writing just yet, although, to be fair, my test play with Chat GPT was better punctuated.[4]

For the second week running, Catherine arrives in class without a working camera or mic. We don't know how to fix it. Her mum asked recently if I recommend an iPad or laptop for classes, so I guess an upgrade is imminent. Most of my students use iPads, but I would recommend a laptop or PC every time – the print is so tiny on so many of our PPT slides or story texts, that the bigger the screen, the better. Why would anyone want to take class on something so tiny as a phone or iPad?

---

4. Since writing this diary entry, generative AI has developed at a frightening speed, impacting much of the creative world in the worst ways. I was surprised, when revisiting this diary, to realise I had ever tried ChatGPT; I have no recollection of doing so. I haven't used any kind of generative AI since that moment, to the best of my knowledge. I am strongly and loudly against the use of generative AI in any part of writing, or the creative industry. ESL teaching is another industry under severe threat from GenAI, as more and more students are subjected to AI 'tutors' instead of living human beings.

Then he goes out or a walk on the street.It seemed so he was invisible.No one has so head on the street.No one had even have a look at him.With his weird coat and his pink dress.Then he walked to the corner of the street.And go straight into the cake shop.And.The cake shop sports. Mrs.MRS, sweetie Head.He did not even look at him.And he take a doughnut and eat it invisibly.And go out from the cake shop.And he, he walks straight.Too.The actual.And he take a look in the actual job.And keep going.He saw a boy riding a bike, and the boy is not so him anyway.He just go past the boy and the boy.Was riding his bike.Even not Pizza.The normal people.The normal people go straight.And turn left.When she turn, there was.

There was a cat.An orange, fluffy cat in the corner.And when the cat.And when the normal people pass the cat.It seemed so the cat had saw him.So the cat chase on.The normal people did not know the cat was chasing him.So keep going.And then.He walk to the supermarket.The supermarket does not let pants.Or animals go in..But the cat steals followed him..And no one has seen the cat.Two, it seemed, so the cat was invisible to.So the cat follow the normal people.The normal people go inside invisibly.And cakes.I'm.And take a piece. Lollipop.From the shop.And then go out without giving.The boss, any money.

It was it. It was another morning.Now.In this invisible and normal people's lives. He keep going.And he goes into a park.And bump into those of peoples.But those peoples did not realize that was the normal people.Who bumped into them.Day.They look around Sicily and.And keep going dumbly.And then.The normal people.Work on some stairs.And the orange cat follow.Followed him.Whenever he walk to a place..Then the normal people.Go into an alley.This alley people.Was all looking at the current.But they can't. They still can't see the normal people.The normal people keep going.He keep going and going.And then he reach a tree.That was a sycamore tree..He climb up and find a watch on it.In China, the watch to the summer morning.

Eight o'clock and a half.And he click on the clock.Then he and the cat had return.To his Hamburger.And some chicken meat, breakfast.And..And the cat had eaten.The hamburger.Then the normal people.And the normal people had no idea..About.So he saw the cat ate the hamburger.And take the cat under the sofa.And look, the cat under the sofa.Then he go to take his pet.I'll write something terrible.Under his desk.Z.

Honey's voice to text story

March

Wednesday March 1st 2023
Number of classes: 5
Number of students: 3+3+2+1+1
Lessons to plan for tomorrow: 1

Wednesdays are generally nice days, with the three literature classes back-to-back.

Sophia gets her class extra homework by saying she thinks *My Father's Dragon* would be more interesting if the main character did not solve all the problems so easily, which I do agree with. So we decide that each of the girls would write a missing chapter, in which the main character meets another animal that has not been mentioned in the story. The new animal will cause a problem, and Elmer (the character) has nothing left in his backpack to deal with the problem. The girls must decide what he will do. This is such a great class as the girls have some really gritty conversations each week.

I have a message telllling me a past student wants to return, but can only do 8 P.M. classes, and I have no space for her. I am holding 8 P.M. Monday for the new beginners in April, but now I'm wondering if I should ditch them and accept a return of lovely Cherrie.

Later, Buse and I resort to our old favourite of trading Shakespearean insults, but in a less cheery class straight after, Mira updates me on the earthquake situation in Turkiye. Search and rescue efforts have been stopped (it has been almost a month since the event on 6th February). She tells me that for many years, a major earthquake has been predicted to decimate Istanbul, but that no plans have been put in place to deal with this. We Google around a bit, and she is right. It is expected that at some point in the next twenty years, a major earthquake will occur. Istanbul has a greater population than the whole of Ireland and is the heart of Turkiye. It has a mix of old historic buildings and newer buildings, none of which are built to withstand an earthquake. Over 50,000 people have died in February's earthquake. The impact of an Istanbul earthquake would bring Turkiye to its knees.

Thursday March 2nd 2023
Number of classes: 3
Number of students: 3+3+4
Lessons to plan for tomorrow: 1

Unusually for a Thursday, my third class is calmer and a bit subdued. Maybe because the lesson is harder and they donn't understand the topic well enough to have their usual amount of fun, or maybe because Luffy is ill and doesn't talk so much. In a mid-lesson twist, Zoom does something weird and the class vanishes, but even this is no great excitement as I simply restart it and the students come back. A nothing-y kind of day, then, except for Language Linkers checking in to see what availability I have for a new refugee class.

Friday March 3rd 2023
Number of classes: 5
Number of students: 2+2+4+1+1
Lessons to plan for Monday: 1

I'm not sad that Belle and Kim's course ended today. It's been one of the tougher courses, due to a combination of sporadic attendance on Kim's part and a tedious mix of drop-in trial students, leading to a lack of continuity in, well, everything! But Belle is already doing another new course with me on Wednesdays and can no longer fit this Friday time slot into her busy schedule, and Kim... Well, Kim is Kim.

MONDAY MARCH 6TH 2023
NUMBER OF CLASSES: 3
NUMBER OF STUDENTS: 1+2+2
LESSONS TO PLAN FOR TOMORROW: 1

I had a message yesterday to give me a long list of class updates, among which was one to say Mia will join the first class today, and Alice the second class. Neither show up. But at least that makes the classes easy, despite realising that Apple doesn't really know what a map is or how to use one, and the lesson being based entirely on the assumption that the students know what a map is and what maps are for.

The message also said that Kim and Belle's Friday class will not restart, and Kim is going to join the last few weeks of another course. Which is a bit annoying as that class is a great tight-knit group who are working very well, and often independently, and Kim won't have the background knowledge to pick up and slot in.

Tuesday March 7th 2023
Number of classes: 4
Number of students: 1+2+4+2
Lessons to plan for tomorrow: 3

Catherine has a lovely new laptop, to help her solve the connection issues, but it doesn't work as she still only manages to stay connected for small chunks of the class, and in most of that time, I can neither see nor hear her. In good news, Mango has had great connection for the last few weeks. I introduce them to a half-naked David Bowie as we start Part 2 of *Wonder* today, where Via (a character) references 'Space Oddity'. They've never heard of Bowie, so we look at a selection of photos and listened to the song twice.

Kayley's silkworms have grown, and are no more appealing than they were when they were smaller, However, at least last time, they were a useful classroom prop and teaching aid. Today, they are just a distraction. Apple, once again, has no time for imagination today, but by the end of the class I've already forgotten why and am kicking myself for not writing it down.

WEDNESDAY MARCH 8TH 2023
NUMBER OF CLASSES: 6
NUMBER OF STUDENTS: 3+3+2+1+1+1
LESSONS TO PLAN FOR TOMORROW: 1

Buse has decided she is no longer interested in the welfare of turtles. They, she informs me, have gone too far this time. Their crime is that McDonalds have switched their plastic straws for paper ones, which taste funny. Buse, however, owns a reusable metal straw, and has realised she could bring it along in future. She also hasn't vaped all day, which is good, and has told her friends to stop too, which is better. Meanwhile, she is considering marijuana. She is thirteen.

Mira and I spend much of the class sharing illicit (according to the platform/company we meet through) personal information as I tried to work out how to send her a book to her Turkish address. On a shared screen, she sees the entire details of my Amazon account including bank card info, and I type in her address. None of which would be approved of by the company. Even then, Amazon doesn't recognise the address, so our breach of rules is futile. (I've known Mira for about five years now, so we have a certain level of trust.)

Thursday March 9th 2023
Number of classes: 3
Number of students: 3+3+4
Lessons to plan for tomorrow: 0

The message I had earlier in the week has so far been wrong on nearly all counts. None of the extra students have turned up. Kim does not appear in the class I expected him in today. The new Zoom ID I was sent for the 7 p.m. class does not get me into the class because it is actually the new Zoom ID for a totally different class. (*Try this one instead*, they say, and send me the old ID number, which works.)

I thought I had a class to prepare for tomorrow then remember that Amy and Lindsey have postponed till Monday, so that's nice. I love a cancelled or postponed class – and that's not even sarcasm. I'm always grateful for a free hour, and even though I don't need to prepare their lesson, I do it anyway. I want to prep my other Monday classes too, but I haven't been sent the files yet, so looks like I'll still be working on Sunday.

FRIDAY MARCH 10TH 2023
NUMBER OF CLASSES: 2
NUMBER OF STUDENTS: 4+1
LESSONS TO PLAN FOR MONDAY: 1 (BUT SEE ABOVE. I CAN'T DO IT BECAUSE I'M WAITING FOR A FILE: 'I'LL SEND IT ON SATURDAY.')

Today is a remarkably unexciting day. Kim and Belle's class is finished, and we have no replacement class for their time slot yet. Lindsey and Amy have postponed until Monday. Mira messages to say she's sick.

In the only morning class left, the students are all tired. They are young, and their class is 8 P.M. (Beijing time) on a Friday, so it's never a surprise when they are tired. Jerry only turns up hallway through. We are taking a mid-class break and I've turned my camera off to encourage them to move away from the screens and have a stretch, when I suddenly realise Jerry is there, so that's the end of my break while I bring him up to speed.

Buse asks for help on a school project about Malala Yousafzai but when I offer her a suggestion, she says she's already submitted it to the teacher. We still can't beat the Impossible Quiz, and just as I lose my last life, we run out of class time.

Monday March 13th 2023
Number of classes: 4
Number of students: 1+2+2+2
Lessons to plan for tomorrow: 1

Sky and Apple's classes are probably the most fun classes I have all week at present, although the Thursday Luffy/Cynthia/Vincent/Bryan combination is a close second.

Today's first sidetrack takes us down a fruit route, and into a discussion about raspberries versus strawberries, and starts from Sky showing me a pot of cream (or something) that he says had raspberries in it. Then, in the break, Apple's little sister appears in her usual noisy way and I ask Apple (again!) what her sister's name is. The reason I never remember, Apple explains, is that she doesn't have an English name, because she doesn't go to school. Once we get round Apple's ongoing difficulty with 'what if' or 'when', and she stops saying that the sister doesn't go to school, Apple and Sky explain that when a child goes to English classes, that's when they get an English name. Sky tells me his teacher chose his name, but then admits that his mum *is* his English teacher. Apple's mum chose 'Apple' because when Apple was smaller, her face was round like an apple. It's a name that suits her very well, but she informs us with a very straight face that now her face is not like an apple anymore, she wants her mum to change her name to Banana. Luckily, she isn't serious and bursts into laughter after Sky and I both say 'Banana' in equally horrified voices. "Don't change your name to Banana," we say. And then we go to the whiteboard to draw up a list of other bad names:

Watermelon, Plate, Hula Hoop. All bad round names.

Cherry, Apple, Sunny: good round names.

Then we move on, and Apple suggests calling her sister 'Homework People' or 'Cute Baby'. Hmm. Maybe not the first, at least. Sky, meanwhile, tells us he has a very fat girl in his class at school who is, in fact, called Banana. But I'm not entirely certain if he is telling the truth.

In my second company lesson, Rain and Xika are so well-prepared that they both realise I have loaded the wrong lesson today, and tell me which one we need! Lucky they noticed, as I would have gone blindly on. Shame they aren't so great at character description, but at least they are observant!

Lindsey and Amy have their postponed-from-Friday lesson today, culminating our three weeks of talking about *The Big Breakfast*[1] and being a servant. Both choose the jobs they think were easiest (powdering wigs and making butter) and

---

1. Hunt, R and Brychta, A, *The Big Breakfast*, Oxford University Press, 2007

the jobs they think were hardest (cleaning fireplaces) to write about. Although I don't even mention that I have open fireplaces to clean, both decline my suggestion that they fly to Ireland and become my servants, so a disappointing end to our lessons about servants.

TUESDAY MARCH 14TH 2023
NUMBER OF CLASSES: 3
NUMBER OF STUDENTS: 1+2+2
LESSONS TO PLAN FOR TOMORROW: 2

It's refreshing to only have Kate and Honey in the 6 P.M. BJT class now, although I doubt it'll last. These two are well-matched and have great comprehension and speaking skills so we get to have in-depth conversations and not have to re-explain or simplify for Angelia. However, that Angelia has dropped both her classes for now won't help her improve, and when she has time to start up again, she'll be even further back.

Kate and Honey and I spend a large part of class exploring generating ideas, and seeing how one idea can lead to another. Kate makes a neat story map, complete with its basics, but lacking in extra details. Honey hasn't made hers yet, but I imagine when she does, it will be a lot more like the ones I make, with all kinds of tangents.

In Catherine and Mango's class, Catherine has the recurring issues with her sound and camera, but she says in the chat box that she can hear me, so I set them a long writing task and let them work independently. We're about halfway through *Wonder* now.

These literature classes are very enjoyable, but as they are all new, there's a lot of preparation each week. Tomorrow, we continue with *A Pig Named Mercy*[2] and *James and the Giant Peach*, and begin *Because of Winn-Dixie*[3].

I only have the *James* lesson left to prepare, but now I also have seventeen new files for a new course to go through and order.

---

2. DiCamillo, K, *A Piglet Named Mercy*, Walker books, 2019

3. DiCamillo, K, *Because of Winn-Dixie*, Walker Books, 2000

Wednesday March 15th 2023
Number of classes: 6
Number of students: 3+3+2+1+1
Lessons to plan for tomorrow: 1

I task Harry and Susie with imagining what else the travellers on the Giant Peach may have seen (or been otherwise aware of) as they travelled through the clouds. Susie imagines flowers, but gives little detail other than that the travellers smelled them but did not see them. Harry, meanwhile, assures us that the clouds are made from floating milk, produced by cows who live on the clouds. (We don't get into the chicken/egg question of how the first clouds were made for the cows to live on to produce new clouds, but I am absolutely sold on the idea of cloud-dwelling cows and swirling, floating milk clouds. I, while they work on their own imaginings, imagine a cloud-based ice cream stall, with an Einstein-haired vendor selling wafer cones stuffed with pastel-hued cloud. Yum.

We then have a discussion about peach travel vs plane travel. Harry, unsurprisingly, would prefer to travel by peach. Susie, equally unsurprisingly, would not.

Thursday 16th March 2023
Number of classes: 3
Number of students: 3+3+4
Lessons to plan for tomorrow: 1

Craig is in the car, as usual, and once again, he has no paper or pen.

Kevin and Alice are both late.

I am busy adapting the class to suit Craig's situation, by deciding to show the video first, so he can watch in the car without need of writing anything. I have just finished explaining this, and hit 'play' on the video, when Kevin arrives, so I stop the video, brief Kevin on what information we are watching for in the video, hit play, and Alice arrives. Repeat. Except, after I tell Alice all this information, Craig is almost home; all students are in class, and the whole point of starting with the video is lost. As are the first ten minutes of class.

This class is well-behaved and fun, but today I need to remind them of two main rules:

1. **Get to class on time.**

2. **Bring a pen or pencil and a notebook, given that this is a writing class.**

It shouldn't be this hard.

By the time the third class has started, noisily, chaotically, and with many repeats of 'What can you see now, Bryan?', my voice is barely holding up. They are livelier than ever, but not in a good way – they usually at least pay vague levels of attention to the class. We do, however, establish that Bryan travels to school by space rocket, and Luffy has a Pumpkin Spaceship. Both of which are far more exciting to discuss than the textbook about 'our nation' (aka none of our nations, but that only-nation-in-the-centre-of-the-world nation, the U S of A.) To paraphrase Luffy, we don't give a stuffed pumpkin about *our nation*'s Thanksgiving. Luffy, meanwhile, offers his disparaging view that he doesn't like America because they made the Indians leave. I can't disagree, although my own nation's history of colonisation is equally bad (I'm British, and we were probably the *worst* offenders.)

Friday 17th March 2023
Number of classes: 4
Number of students: 2+4+1+1
Lessons to plan for Monday: 1

Today is St Patrick's Day. The last bank holiday we had was on my birthday in February. On both of these days, the rest of

Ireland rests, sleeps, parties, plays. I, meanwhile, work. It is not a holiday in China, or in Turkiye, where today's students live.

In the few minutes while I am in the Zoom class before class starts, with my camera and mic off, I can see Amy dancing in her living room. The minute class starts, she disappears, and then has endless connection issues throughout the entire class.

In the next class, Sean falls asleep in the break. It's been a while since a student fell asleep, but the boys in this class are my youngest students. Sean and Bourne are only four or five years old, and the class is from 8 P.M. until 9 P.M. in their time zone. When I taught more younger classes, falling asleep was a common occurrence. Amy and I still laugh about her first classmate, Emily, from about three years ago, who fell asleep in almost every class. Amy is seven now, and can't imagine anyone sleeping in class these days.

Later: My 13-year-old Turkish student has just informed me that many girls in her year group are or have been pregnant. I am rarely speechless with Buse, not when she tells me about vaping, or burning her arm in a dare, or any of the other crazy things she does, but at this, I am speechless. And shocked, and worried.

Monday 20th March 2023
Number of classes: 5
Number of students: 1+2+2+1+1
Lessons to plan for tomorrow: 1

This morning, Sky spends the first five minutes of class telling me how ugly my dog is while we wait for Apple to reconnect after having appeared briefly and then getting cut off. Poor Wilf – he may not be the tidiest dog with his overgrown sheep-style coat, but he's far from ugly. I don't know why Sky says this, except in continuation of the ongoing assertion in this class that even the cutest baby animal is ugly, but as soon as Apple re-appears, Wilf is forgotten and the hilarity of them reading a story in characters' voices takes over. Apple seems to think that ANY character's voice must be as high-pitched and skin-crawling as fingernails on a blackboard, but to be fair, skin-crawling aside, they do it very well.

Later: Oops. Having rescheduled Buse's Wednesday and Friday classes this week to compensate for going away on Wednesday, I then forget to turn up at the right time. Luckily, I log on at five past three 'just to check' and she is calling and I am only minutes late. I was sure we'd scheduled for our usual 3.30 p.m. time, but we obviously agreed on half an hour earlier. Mira doesn't turn up for the lesson straight after (although she had never confirmed her rearranged lesson) so at least running five minutes late with Buse doesn't have any domino effect.

Tuesday 21st March 2023
Number of classes: 4
Number of students: 1+2+3+1
Lessons to plan for Monday: 0

Kayley, Eric, and Apple begin a new course today. Following my advice that their previous course was a bit hard, we have made a new course for these students. Today we 'read' two stories without words. It goes even better than I had anticipated, with the three students working well to tell the story of a woman who wanted pancakes for breakfast using great detail. Apple, it seems, loves the smell of a cowshed and warm milk, but thinks the chicken house would smell so awful she never wants to eat another egg in her life. Kayley helpfully points out that eggs are chickens' babies and milk is for calves – as a vegetarian, I silently applaud, but in class terms, it is a sidetrack we could do without. Kayley also produces one of her twelve silkworm cocoons to show us and now I want to raise my own silkworms.

Catherine and Mango both have great internet, full sound and visuals for the entire class, for the first time in ages. It's always a bonus when every single student in a day has no tech issues.

Monday 27th March 2023
Number of classes: 2
Number of students: 2+3
Lessons to plan for tomorrow: 2

It's always nice to have a break[4], but it's always weird to settle back in.

Apple and Sky are on great form, although Apple has her usual struggles with 'if' and speculation. Today's book is the story of the Magic Paintbrush. I ask Apple and Sky what they would paint if they had a magic paintbrush, knowing Apple's response before I even finish the question:

A: "But Teacher ..."

---

4. I had been in England for my grandfather's funeral. Despite it being a funeral, it *was* a nice occasion. My grandpa was 98. He did pretty well. And it's not often all the family is together, in our hometown too, so we really did enjoy ourselves.

Me: "Yes, Apple?" (Resigned voice of prediction.)

A: "I don't have a magic paintbrush."

Me, internally: Of course you bloody don't. Aloud: "Apple, you are not good at 'if'. I know you don't have a magic paintbrush but IF you did ..."

In a more insightful part of the lesson, however, she offers the empathic and generous view that we should not judge the bad guys on the strength of their looks, and the wolf may not be the baddie just because he is ugly. This from the girl who said squirrels and baby rabbits are ugly, too. I am pleased that she is not swayed by looks alone in her character judgements.

In the second class, Xika and Rain are joined by a new student. She settles in beautifully and although she is only six, communicates fluently and writes well too.

During the break, Rain takes his iPad into a bedroom, and shows us his new brother. The baby is about a month old, but this is the first I knew of his arrival! Rain's dad is lying on the bed with the baby, but luckily fully dressed. Many of my colleagues in the ESL world have had somewhat less-clothed experiences of their students' fathers, but I have never yet seen a naked man on camera, in over five years of this. Or any background shower scenes. There was that one time when a Saudi Arabian grandmother changed her bra, reflected clearly in the mirror hanging over her blissfully-unaware granddaughters' heads as we did the lesson, but that was a long time ago …

Rain's introduction to his baby brother starts a trend, and Xika takes us to see her sister (who we have met before). It's bedtime in China – this class finishes at 8 P.M. BJT, and Xika's sister is also lying on a bed, their mother curled next to her in her nightwear. Xika's mother is not enthused to be caught on camera, and in great English, sends Xika packing straight back to her class space.

We are reading *A Piglet Named Mercy* in this class, and today is focussed on discussing setting and character. In this story, Mercy jumps from the slaughter truck. *Slaughter* and *truck* are not words these low-level 6–8-year-olds know, but they manage to explain very well why Mercy chose to jump from the 'car':

The question I ask is why she jumped and how this shows she is clever and brave.

Rain: "She does not want to be a hamburger." Great summary, Rain.

Tuesday 28th March 2023
Number of classes: 5
Number of students: 1+2+3+2+1
Lessons to plan for tomorrow: 3

Kayley's silkworms have transformed! Last week they were cocoons, but today, she has moths. The grand reveal went something like this:

Me: "Oh! Wow! Moths!"

K: "Butterflies."

Me: "I'm so amazed! They are gorgeous! I love them. Moths."

K: "Butterflies."

Me: "Apple! Look! Kayley's silkworms have changed into moths!"

A: "Butterflies."

And so on.

They are pretty awesome though. Something I have noticed over the years is that all my students pronounce 'can' and 'can't' in exactly the same way as each other. So when Kayley plucks a moth from the box and balances it on the tip of her finger, and I ask why it doesn't fly away, it is either because it can't, or because it can, and that's the only answer I get.

In a random moment of insanity, I have just answered a message asking if I can fit in a new Turkish girl on the conversational platform, as in the platform that pays next to nothing, by saying *maybe* instead of *no*. I have neither the inclination nor the need. But on the other hand, Buse needs to swap from Friday to Tuesday so to sit at my laptop for thirty minutes for her, I may as well try to tag another student before or after her to make it worth the bother.

Wednesday 29th March 2023
Number of classes: 7
Number of students: 1+3+3+2+1+1+1
Lessons to plan for tomorrow: 1

I get up early today (well, not really, but because British Summer Time just began at the weekend, it feels early!) because I only prepared two of today's lessons yesterday and have one more to do still, so although as I write this I have only met with Dorrie so far, I'm already yawning.

Dorrie and I take a nice break from our Harry Potter marathon – we've been reading Harry for almost three years now, thirty minutes, twice a week. It took a little over two years to read the first book. We started the second a few months ago, and it's both quicker and slower than the first! Dorrie reads with a lot more confidence and accuracy, and I need to help her less, but on the other hand there are more complex words in this book and the reading level is higher. She sometimes tires, and trips over even easier words, so we often intersperse it with clips from the film to match the part we are reading. But today, she tells me that tomorrow, she is going on a class trip to do something. She doesn't know the English, so she types the characters into the chat box:

蓝染

The translation gives me a word I don't know, which doesn't help. We put the Chinese into Google and come up with beautiful images of either tie-dye or batik, all in blues and whites, and the impression that it is a Japanese form of one of these techniques. With a few minutes of videos of each, Dorrie thinks it is tie-dye she will be doing, but it's left me with an urge to try batik: a process I've never attempted.

After class, I do a little more research, and in Google, although Google recognise the characters as the Chinese word pronounced as 'Lánrǎn', the implication is that it is a Japanese 'thing', as all the definitions below the translation refer to Japanese. The word translates to English as Aizen, also referred to as Aizome, or indigo dyeing. This, then, explains why every picture showed blue dye, and perhaps the technique refers more to the colour of the dye than the process used. I hope

Dorrie remembers to bring her dyed fabric to show me next week.

In my first company class, my electricity cuts out just long enough to disconnect my internet. In previous years, when I worked for different companies, this would constitute a full-blown panic and the knowledge that I would lose pay over it. Today, I calmly send a message, stroll downstairs to reboot my internet on my emergency back-up system, stroll back up to my office and reconnect. Only to discover that when I got bumped from the classroom, one of the students had been allocated as host, and I now can't unmute myself or share the screen until we have gone through many minutes of charades to explain that she is in charge and has to fix everything for us to continue. Nonetheless, it is funny rather than stressful, and reminds me once again how lucky I am with the company I currently work for.

Later, another technical issue loses me a class on the conversational platform. They are Beta-testing a new classroom layout, and Mira and I, dropped into it two minutes apart (I was a bit late due to the ongoing issue that same platform imposes on almost every lesson with Buse), could not meet. Mira, having left the class to wait for me, isn't allowed back in, and I, having got in, am not allowed to leave it to try to restart to let her in ... My thirty minutes of pay has turned into twenty minutes of typing a report to submit to hopefully regain my lost pay and Mira her lost minutes. These are the parts of the job I hate.

Meanwhile over on Facebook, a lengthy discussion is brewing on a writing group about the use of different Englishes. It's interesting and informative and I imagine the moderators will shut it down soon before it gets any more political or contentious. I never cease to be amazed at the lack of tolerance from some (white, English or American, usually) people towards those who use English to communicate on these groups, effectively but often grammatically incorrectly, in a second language. The Original Poster has been slated for poor English, despite it clearly not being his first language, and a group of usually well-mannered people has descended in mockery and ridicule. I see this among other ESL teachers too, so I don't know why I'm so surprised to see it in my writing group.

Friday 31st March 2023
Number of classes: 2
Number of students: 2+4
Lessons to plan for Monday: 2

I wake up to a discombobulating message about a child who will join my G2B Writing class. It takes me a while to work out which class the message refers to, as next week is the penultimate lesson in the G2B course so I can't equate the message to this class. While I understand that new students like to try courses, it's never a good idea to throw a child into a course at lesson 15 of 16. Nonetheless, I respond to instruct the child to watch the video we discussed in yesterday's class as this is where we will pick up from next week. Then I realise I may as well ask Craig to watch it to, since he was sick yesterday and missed the lesson.

The conversation goes as follows:

Me: *He should watch the video 'One Man Band' from Lesson 30 (yesterday's class).*

Me: *Actually, please can you ask Craig to be sure to watch it too before next Thursday.*

Fiona: *OK*

Fiona: *Craig may ask for a leave today. He is having a fever now.*

Me (panicking and frantically checking my schedule and the date): *That was yesterday!*

Me (still not entirely certain as to which day it is today): *He doesn't have class today.*

F: *I got a brain fever!*

Phew. Panic over.

As is March.

April

Monday 3rd April 2023
Number of classes: 4
Number of students: 1+2+3+2
Lessons to plan for tomorrow: 1

I meet my new beginners today for the first time. I had totally forgotten how much *mess* beginner students make. By the time I'm done, I have five packs of flashcards emptied out and spread all over the desk, thoroughly mixed up. One of my big puppets is on the floor, sulking, no doubt, at being mis-named. It's so long since I used them I forgot that the orange one is called Toby and the blue one is called Max, and now I'll have to continue with calling them Sam (orange) and Toby (blue) forever with these students. And hope my dog called Sam never bothers to show his face while I'm talking to this pair. (Shouldn't be problem, as he gave up the will to meet students on camera years ago.)

One of the new girls is only three, not four as her mother told me, and barely speaks throughout the class. Meanwhile, just off-camera, their mother and father speak a *lot*. It's useful for a parent to stay close when the children are this young, but I could do without both parents repeating everything I say. I'll let the girls settle in before I ease the parents out of the classroom. The older one has better English than I'd expected, which makes it easier than if they are absolute beginners with zero English. She knows numbers, colours, and many basic nouns, so there's a good base to start from.

Rain and Xika also have a new classmate today. He is very able, and well-matched to Xika, but unfortunately this just makes Rain look even less like he's making any progress at all.

Tuesday 4th April 2023
Number of classes: 4
Number of students: 1+1+4+2+1
Lessons to plan for tomorrow: 3

My days with the conversational platform have been numbered since they've updated the classrooms, badly. It's a great platform to start out on, and after five years or so in ESL, I've built up enough other, better-paying classes to not need this platform anymore. I only keep on it for four long-term regulars who I meet with for about 3-4 hours a week. The pay is abysmal – less than a quarter of what I get elsewhere, but it's easy enough.

Was. *Was* easy enough.

The update has taken away the flexibility and added extra levels of work. I can see it will help those who use the platform as their sole gig, but for me, who uses it so minimally, it now puts more effort on me to watch the time and enter the classroom, whereas before, I would stay busy until I heard the ringtone. Now, if one student runs late, I can no longer send a quick message asking the next to call a few minutes late, as they will lose their allocated minutes for not starting on time, and I will lose the corresponding pay. I have direct contact for all four students after knowing them for so long, so now is the moment to try to persuade them to come to me privately. This, in theory, is unethical, and in terms of the agreement with the platform, very much not allowed, but after five years of $5 for a 30-minute class, and being professional, loyal, and reliable for all that time, I owe them nothing. I meet Dorrie, and we Harry-Potter through another thirty minutes, but with the gnawing knowledge that I won't be meeting her here for much longer.

In my first company class, Kate is absent, giving Honey a most useful one-to-one class in which we analyse her writing carefully and work on the thing she struggles with – writing her ideas down fast enough! I can relate to this – before I fell asleep last night, I had a plethora of great ideas for what I know would have been contest-worthy short stories. Not wanting to put the light on, I wrote no notes, despite knowing I would be unlikely to remember a thing come morning. Honey is the same – her creativity is boundless, but her ability to capture every idea on paper is limited. I give her the advice I should give myself: WRITE IT DOWN. Neither of us will heed this advice.

In the second company class, Kayley continues to fail to understand how to write a sentence, even when directed to copy from the screen. Today she produces:

1. **in the bath**

2. **Kayley in the bath. splashes**

Even on the occasions when I give in and script the complete sentence for her to copy in full, she usually copies the wrong thing. I'm not sure how to fix this. In better news, her silk moths are enormous and look a bit like miniature owls. I wouldn't want them flying around my house, let alone balancing on the end of my finger.

Wednesday 5th April 2023
Number of classes: 6
Number of students: 3+2+2+1+1+1
Lessons to plan for tomorrow: 1

In our G3 Literature class, things get heavy. We are reading *Because of Winn-Dixie*, in which Gloria Dump is a recovering alcoholic and Otis an ex-prisoner. Honey and Sophia are seven or eight (it was Sophia's birthday yesterday). I ask them if they understand why Gloria showed Opal the bottle tree in her garden, and an in-depth discussion about alcoholism ensues. Honey's grandfather, she explains, with understanding, often gets drunk. He sways and staggers. She demonstrates with action. Her uncle, moreover, is an actual alcoholic. Deep, for a lunchtime chat with a pair of young children.

I find a cheat for the conversational platform that has made the changes I'm frustrated with. By opening the platform in two separate windows, I am able to connect to Buse and Mira at the same time for a minute overlap in their classes. It would be more fun if Mira could hear Buse, but I only realise after I disconnect Buse that all I'd needed to do was remove my headphones and it probably would've worked. I feel too guilty blatantly breaking rules to keep it going, so I still lose a minute of pay and Buse a minute of her class time, but it is a hack worth discovering. What's the worst that can happen? I don't care if they 'sack' me as it's no longer a hassle I need. I have contact info for all the students anyway.

THURSDAY 6TH APRIL 2023
NUMBER OF CLASSES: 3
NUMBER OF STUDENTS: 3+3+4
LESSONS TO PLAN FOR TOMORROW: 0 (DONE IT!)

Yesterday, I confirmed whether the 8 P.M. company class today would continue – they finished their course last week. Yes, I was told. It will. Today, two of the class don't arrive, and one new child does appear, surprising me and making me lose class time to check who I am actually expecting for the lesson. I have a bit of a strop, reminding them to tell me in advance, not a minute after the class begins. Later, I realise they had not only told me the day before, but also that I had replied to that message. Hashtag mortified. Yes, I send an apology to the company for stropping.

The class doesn't go very well though, and I will miss the old foursome that worked so well.

Friday 7th April 2023
Number of classes: 4
Number of students: 2+4+1+1
Lessons to plan for Monday: 1

The two single 30-minute conversational students do not go to plan, and I get paid for precisely ten minutes of the hour I spend at my computer trying to help them connect. The time has come to break away from this platform for sure. However, in suggesting to Buse that we switch to private lessons, I am shocked by her telling me they only pay the equivalent of €2.57 per 30-minute class. I am paid $6 for her thirty minutes, and $5 for Mira's lessons, so I am surprised their fees don't even cover my pay. It's bad enough working for $5 or $6, but I can't even contemplate working for €2.50, and although we negotiate a bit, her parents' suggestion of €4 for thirty minutes is not worth my while, especially as I would also have processing fees deducted by my bank.

Is this the time to cut these four students loose? I will miss them, as the only reason I have endured this low pay is that I enjoy chatting to these four and have watched them all grow over the last four or five years. Tough decision, but thrown into sharp relief by the fact that my new private, reduced-cost 30-minute beginners class with Yiyi and Xiaorou provides me with the same return as FIVE of these conversational thirty minutes. It should really be a no-brainer.

MONDAY 10TH APRIL 2023
NUMBER OF CLASSES: 3
NUMBER OF STUDENTS: 2+3+2
LESSONS TO PLAN FOR TOMORROW: 1

I ask my company staff if there is a good reason for Xika's grandparents to interrupt our class to take Xika's temperature each week. Today, the temperature-taking leaves us waiting for her to complete her written work long after Winson has finished his. I don't see why they can't do her temperature check before or after, but the response to my message is in sympathy with the family – they are concerned that Xika has a cold.

My new beginners class is quite endearing and I am finally getting the chance to use my big puppets once more – they have been collecting dust for far too long and it's good to see them earning their keep again – they weren't cheap but haven't been used in a very long time as none of my other students are low-level enough to warrant their use. Yiyi is a sweetie and seems genuinely pleased to see me. Her sister, meanwhile, stays long enough to say hello, then vanishes. I hope the parents won't try to renegotiate the price if one of the children doesn't participate.

Tuesday 11th April 2023
Number of classes: 3
Number of students: 2+4+2
Lessons to plan for tomorrow: 3

Kate and Honey have one of my favourite classes today – that in which the students first draw a monster, then develop character profile information about that monster, then write a story based on a problem their monster faces. It is always a class the students enjoy, and as they spend a large chunk of the class-time independently writing, I get to sit and twiddle my thumbs for a good thirty minutes – or write my own monster story. Today, I didn't make a monster, as I've done this a few times before, but it did remind me of my masterpiece about Blanket, produced in a previous class for this same lesson:

Blanket shivered and wrapped his fur around his body. He blinked three of his eyes a few times and looked out at the night sky. The stars twinkled and the moon peeked out from behind a cloud.

Blanket smiled. He knew just how he could warm up a bit. He shuffled from his cave and out onto the rocky mountainside. He placed one of his feet firmly onto a flat rock and with his other two feet, he began to dance. There was no music up here on the mountain, so Blanket had to make his own. "Oooooooooh! Owwww, oooo-ey oooh, umph!" He howled, although the last 'umph' was more about how his foot slipped and he landed heavily on his furry bottom. "Ouch," he grumbled. And so did his stomach. All that dancing had made him very hungry. He shuffled back into his cave, opened the cake tin, and peered inside. His large nose quivered, and drool dripped from his mouth. He shook the tin. He tipped it upside down. He looked again. Nothing made any difference. The tin was empty. Blanket groaned. So did his stomach. "Bother," he said. "I'll have to go and dig up some turnips." He pulled on three thick boots and picked up his spade. The moon shone on the turnip patch. It was a splendid turnip patch. He had painted a wonderful sign: Turnip Patch, and he had polished the smooth rock until it gleamed. It was a wonderful turnip patch. Except for one small problem. It had absolutely no turnips. Not a single one.

One day, perhaps I will finish it, and find out how poor Blanket solves his turnip problem.

WEDNESDAY 12TH APRIL 2023
NUMBER OF CLASSES: 3
NUMBER OF STUDENTS: 3+2+2
LESSONS TO PLAN FOR TOMORROW: 1

It is remarkably blissful not having the conversational classes this week. I have so much spare time and won't see any impact on pay as my new 30-minute Beginners class makes up for the loss of five 30-minute sessions. It feels a lot more like a win than a loss.

Honey and Sophia haven't, unsurprisingly, managed to read the last ten chapters of *Winn-Dixie* for their literature class, so by improvising, and cutting the planned lesson in half, their lesson is also blissful. It's so much nicer to study books at the students' pace than to try to fit a prescribed amount of work into a fixed amount of time. By taking it slower, the girls can actually find time to enjoy the story, which seems to me as if it should be the end goal anyway.

Likewise, in Harry and Susie's class, we have just reached the end of *James and the Giant Peach* after a leisurely thirteen lessons on it plus one extra lesson for Harry in the week Susie couldn't attend. This book is crammed into just four lessons in the company I used to work for. Some of these Chinese students have school for about ten hours a day, then homework and other after school lessons, so to expect them to find time to read several chapters in a second language is a big ask and a sure way to turn them off the pleasure of reading, too.

My third class today is also a literature-based class, and involves an equally well-paced first four chapters of a Minnie and Moo book I'd never heard of, that we all enjoy a lot.[1] Teaching Chinese children about anthropomorphism is always a great class, whichever story I link it to, and today was no exception. Every time I teach this topic, I remember Yuki and Marshall learning how to say the word, and remembering it in every lesson ever after! Those girls were such fun. I wonder what they are doing now.[2]

---

1. *Minnie and Moo: Wanted, Dead or Alive*, Cazet, D, Harper Collins, 2007

2. Yuki and Marshall are students from a few years ago, from a company I worked with before the Chinese online ESL crash. Come to think of it, I did have an email address for one of them. I wonder if it's too late to get in touch after so long.

THURSDAY 13TH APRIL 2023
NUMBER OF CLASSES: 3
NUMBER OF STUDENTS: 3+4+3
LESSONS TO PLAN FOR TOMORROW: 0

In today's final class of our G2B Writing class, I have a new student. I knew he was coming, and he is checking out the class in preparation for joining us in the new G3 course. However, Alice is absent, and Craig is, typically and expectedly late, and Kevin, somewhat predictably is being a total brat. I ask Orlando to introduce himself, and while he is still speaking, but has told us quite a lot of information, Kevin shouts out "Who is O. R. L. A. N. D. O.?" Kevin has also forgotten to bring his work. He continues to interrupt, disrupt, and generally show off until, at last, he starts writing. Even in the writing task, he wants to eschew the instructions and do something entirely different. I have already told him off about six times, in a sterner voice than I usually use in any class, ever. I have never been so pleased to see Craig turn up. I can't imagine Orlando will ever show his face again.

Friday 14th April 2023
Number of classes: 2
Number of students: 2+4
Lessons to plan for Monday: 2

I was wrong about Orlando. He will join the new class. It's another course I've not yet taught for this particular company, so there will be another lesson to do proper prep for each week – as in, although I will be sent files with the lesson, I will rebuild it, correct mistakes, generally tidy it up, and amend it to suit my students and me.

Amy and Lindsey's class is an Oxford Reading Tree lesson where Biff has fun hunting for *animal-died rocks*. This is Amy's made-up phrase for the forgotten correct word: fossil. I like her version better – it explains the object far more clearly.

Susie's mum has requested a whole heap of extras that I generally get away without giving my private students: she asks for a monthly report on Susie's progress and help with preparing for the written part of an upcoming PET test, which I now need to study myself so I can understand what Susie needs.

No matter; I will construct new lessons around it, and luckily, have several of the relevant files from Romanian classes I sometimes cover. In a moment of madness, I've ordered physical copies of books I have as PDFs because if I am actually to use them to make lessons, I prefer to look off-screen for what I need to include. It's a scheme I could do with familiarising myself with anyway, and will add another string to my ESL bow if I can offer PET training. It's a shame that I can't currently even remember what PET means, though.[3]

Monday 17th April 2023
Number of classes: 4
Number of students: 1+2+3+2
Lessons to plan for tomorrow: 1

I meet Dorrie on the going-belly-up conversational platform, and it goes okay, but my time off this platform last week has made me realise that I *will* give it up completely very, very soon, regardless of how well it does or doesn't work.

In our lesson about Mercy Watson (a pig who is treated like a child by the Watsons in the *A Pig Named Mercy* series) Xika and Winson both agree that it's okay to have a pet pig at the kitchen table, although Rain disagrees, but then Xika tells us her friend has a pet jellyfish, so maybe a pig is nothing special.

---

3. Preliminary English Test

Xiaorou and Yiyi, my new beginners, are so excited to see me that they remind me how nice it is to take on beginners. Yiyi only gets slightly confused when I say she is good and she repeats that she is a goat, but the lesson is about farm animals so it's an easy mistake.

Tuesday 18th April 2023
Number of classes: 4
Number of students: 1+2+4+2
Lessons to plan for tomorrow: 2

Kayley is driving me mad.

Even though I structure her sentences on the screen, she still does not write complete sentences. First, despite only having four words to copy, and clear instructions as to WHAT to copy, she writes nothing. By the time Apple and Jolin have written the best part of a whole paragraph, Kayley has still done ... nothing! Then, after going through the whole set of instructions again, it gets little better. For example when I write: **I painted a ......** she copies the dotted line instead of adding a noun. When I explain again, she does not amend the dotted line and add a word, but instead writes a new sentence[4]. She also is reluctant to show her work, and unable to read it accurately. Is it possible she could be dyslexic?

Wednesday 19th April 2023
Number of classes: 6
Number of students: 3+3+2+5+4+5
Lessons to plan for tomorrow: 0

Today is more intense than usual, as I have a lesson to plan from scratch before I start teaching this morning – Harry and Susie will begin *George's Marvellous Medicine*[5] today, and even thought I spent hours last week downloading resources, only one file actually downloaded successfully so I gave up on it. I should have prepared it yesterday, but the sun was shining and I went to see a friend instead, knowing that I had a late enough start this morning to fit it in easily enough. This is straightforward enough, although time-consuming. It takes

---

4. I use the word 'sentence' in the loosest of terms here. I am extremely confident that whatever Kayley wrote, it was *not* a sentence.

5. Dahl, R, *George's Marvellous Medicine*, Jonathan Cape Ltd, 1981

longer to find all those files again than to create the actual lesson.

My other morning classes are smooth and enjoyable too, but today I am beginning a three-day stint of covering the Romanian classes.

Later: The three cover classes go well … ish. I have a nice mix of students I met last time I covered the classes, and a sprinkling of new faces too. The beginner class has made amazing progress. We talk about pirates and they are able to argue with me when I said I want all the treasure. It's always a great sign when the level of communication has progressed enough to allow argument.

In the last of the three classes, I meet with a bunch of teens I met before. Cristi, who was very sad and depressed when I met him a few months back, after a split with his girlfriend, is able to laugh about that now, and is in a far better headspace. In the structured part of the lesson, I show them the wrong video clip, which, we eventually realise, explains why none of them know the answers to the questions. The talk revolves around AirBnB, strangers, and escape rooms. Cristi shares an experience where he punched a guy in a bar who harassed his friend (a girl, who said 'No' to said harasser). We are all suitably impressed. This world needs more Cristis, although he says the policeman didn't agree. (The policewoman, however, did.)

Thursday 20th April 2023
Number of classes: 2
Number of students: 4+8
Lessons to plan for tomorrow: 1

I have an almost day off today – just one Chinese class at 1 p.m. and one Romanian class at 4.30 p.m. The sun is shining and the day is warm, so I've already spent a while in the polytunnel planting out seedlings and checking on the hens, plus written a tricky missing chapter of my current novel before logging on for the 1 o'clock class, in which I am now awaiting my students.

Yesterday, while covering the Romanian classes, their organiser asked if I would be interested in facilitating adult groups in the future – not teaching, she said, just guiding conversations as needed. I'm not, really, but I found myself telling her I'm free in the afternoons anyway. I already know I won't want to do this, especially not for the pay this company gives (approximately half of what my Chinese company pays), even though in theory it's a lot less work. These last two weeks with none of the conversational classes have been lovely, and I've clarified that I don't really need to do any afternoon teaching unless it's really worthwhile. I may tell her I'd be more interested in taking on one of the middle school age groups, or a teen group, as they are kind of fun and also very easy.

FRIDAY 21ST APRIL 2023
NUMBER OF CLASSES: 4
NUMBER OF STUDENTS: 2+4+4+5
LESSONS TO PLAN FOR MONDAY: 1

The Romanian classes have been lovely! The students have, on the whole, been pleasingly happy to see me again, and the classes are such low level prep and delivery that it makes them easy and rewarding. The Beginners class uses a program that is truly the most hideous teaching program I have ever witnessed, that was probably made using the most basic computer software known to man – PAINT circa 1960, perhaps. It has the worst soundtrack ever, and relies heavily on exclaiming everything. Nonetheless, the children seem to learn something from it, although I suspect they'd learn just as much from a cereal packet. It is a high-energy class, with all the bright colours and screamy audio, but the students are fun. Nonetheless, today's Beginner class zaps my stamina and it is far more conducive to my Friday afternoon energy levels to play an online Pictionary style game with the teen group for the last twenty minutes of their two-hour class.

I must be doing okay, as I've been asked to cover for another teacher this coming Friday, too.

MONDAY 24TH APRIL 2023
NUMBER OF CLASSES: 4
NUMBER OF STUDENTS: 1+2+3+2
LESSONS TO PLAN FOR TOMORROW: 1

Today brings hellish classes.

Rain and Xika both have people in their houses who talk pretty much non-stop through the lesson. Xika, who is about seven, gets at least as annoyed as I do, and although I know no Chinese beyond "hello," I can say with absolute conviction that she is yelling at various members of her family to shut the **** up, as am I, albeit internally. She is unsuccessful. Rain doesn't even try to shut his up.

Yiyi and Xiaorou's mum had messaged to ask if we could start their class twenty minutes late, as they would be on the high-speed train at our usual lesson time, which she recognised would make the lesson difficult. Nice to have an aware parent

... until ... when they log on said twenty minutes later, they are in a car.

Days like this are hard work and leave me feeling like I've been shouting into a very windy day in the fog to a dog who has already gone home and is waiting on the doorstep with his feet up.

TUESDAY 25TH APRIL 2023
NUMBER OF CLASSES: 4
NUMBER OF STUDENTS: 1+2+4+2
LESSONS TO PLAN FOR TOMORROW: 3

Kate has been gently persuaded that writing an entire book (well, three sections, an introduction and conclusion over a four-week period) about *jelly* is probably unrealistic. It was bad enough last week when I thought she meant jam, but the clarification that she did in fact mean jelly – the wobbly, British kind – left me with even more limited advice for her other than, "Er, Kate, are you *sure* this is something you can write about for the next few weeks?" She has, thankfully, decided to write about Hong Kong instead. Honey, meanwhile, is still planning her book on home decorating. Where *do* they get their ideas from?

In the second of my company classes, I am amazed to see how different the other three students are without Kayley slowing the lesson to almost-backwards. We sail through the first half of the lesson, with even slow-writer Eric whizzing through sentence after sentence. Everyone added heaps of details; Apple and Jolin get very creative with adding lengthy predicates, and we even almost run according to my scheduled timings.

And then, just as we stop for the break, Kayley arrives.

Eventually, in desperation, I ask Apple to explain in Chinese that when I write: **First I go to the bakery. Then .....** I do NOT want Kayley to write **Then .....**, dots and all, but to add her own ideas to complete the sentence. We've been battling this for weeks now, and I've got nowhere. As Apple explains in Chinese, I think I see a lightbulb come on over Kayley's head. Sure enough, she writes an actual, self-created sentence – all right, not exactly a sentence in all senses of the word, but at least a vaguely coherent collection of words that came together to create an almost-comprehensible idea. Yes! A breakthrough.

And then as the rest of the class writes their **Last ....** sentence, Kayley writes nothing, and the light bulb has faded away to dark once more.

As I am dragging Mango and Catherine through another *Wonder*-based lesson – the book Catherine's mum insisted on, despite it being about 3 levels above their ability – Amy's mum messages to let me know that after about three years of teaching Amy, she needs to stop her lessons for the time being to focus on school exams. It's hard to lose students I've known so long, but the more pressing question is whether will Lindsey continue without her classmate, and if so, how will I find her a new partner to share the class cost? I don't want to continue with the class for half the pay, even if that half-pay value is still an hourly rate I was happy with a couple of years ago!

WEDNESDAY 26TH APRIL 2023
NUMBER OF CLASSES: 4
NUMBER OF STUDENTS: 3+3+2+1
LESSONS TO PLAN FOR TOMORROW: 1

In the first company class, we learn that Nate the Great[6] loves pancakes, and therefore we could all be detectives too, because we also all like pancakes.

In the second, Sophia – and oh my god, this girl thinks like a writer – wants to know how *Love that Dog*[7] got published.

---

6. Weinman Sharmat, M, *Nate the Great*, Coward, McGann & Geoghegan, 1972

7. Creech, S, *Love that Dog*, Bloomsbury, 2001

Not because she doesn't think it good, but because it's so different from the norm. She seems genuinely bewildered, and she's not even in the soul-destroying position I'm currently in of querying literary agents. I tell her I'll try to find out, but I don't get far in my search.

The highlights of the day, though, are:

- Harry telling me that even though it's the May holiday next week, he really wants to have class anyway. This is a big turnaround from when he was partnered with Sean and obviously bored.

- Mira: "Is there an English word for *insert incomprehensible Turkish word here*?" Me: "I dunno! You're the bilingual one."

THURSDAY 27TH APRIL 2023
NUMBER OF CLASSES: 3
NUMBER OF STUDENTS: 3+3+4
LESSONS TO PLAN FOR TOMORROW: 0

Scrolling through my contacts searching for a new classmate for Lindsey, I find Iris. Iris was one of my favourites from the old days of Whales English, before the change to Chinese online classes kicked in and pulled the big companies under, leaving thousands of ESL tutors jobless in the space of a couple of hours.

Iris is vivacious and chatty and cheerful and fun. She is a bit more advanced than Lindsey, but they are a similar age and I feel they will get on well in class together. Iris will probably be good for Lindsey and encourage her to grow in her own ability. Iris's mum is delighted at the idea, and suggests we study *George's Marvellous Medicine* – a course I was planning to suggest to Lindsey's mum anyway. I'm already making this course for Harry and Susie, and when I taught Iris before, she was at the same level as those two, so it feels instinctively like a good plan. I hope Lindsey's mum agrees.

I'll have all of May one-to-one with Lindsey, so need to use it wisely to bring her up to level. I would usually charge more for one-to-one classes, but in the circumstances, that seems unfair, so I'll take the hit and remind myself it's still more than I used to get per hour, and more for fifty minutes than the Romanian classes pay for a full hour.

In Romanian classes news, I received this series of messages today, regarding the classes I am covering tomorrow:

Jimmy told me he just finished the Our World Starters book last lesson. They have also just completed Oxford Phonics 1 and

2 but as Jimmy did not give me advanced notice I do not have the materials uploaded for Oxford Phonics 3 on the drive nor do the parents have the book to print!!!

So I am a bit of a loss as to what you should teach in that class tomorrow!! Can you do an improvised lesson on Phonics??

Jimmy should have let me know at least a week ago he needed new materials sending to the parents!!! Arghh

My immediate response was *er, no, not really* but I replaced it with *I'll wing it,* because frankly, for the lower pay these classes bring, I'm not putting a whole load of prep time into making an entire lesson for someone who should be more organised.

Friday 28th April 2023
Number of classes: 5
Number of students: 2+4+4+3+5
Lessons to plan for Monday: 0

Today is Amy's last day. Her mum comes on camera to say goodbye, and to explain that Amy needs to learn more grammar to prepare for her exams. I hate teaching grammar because it's very boring and I'd have to learn the rules before I was able to teach it well anyway and who has time for that?

I'm sad to see Amy go after so many years but also curious to see how Lindsey will progress without Amy – Lindsey is higher level, and while it's not fair to say Amy has been holding her back, it is true that I've not been able to push Lindsey much. With her new partner — Iris — staring in June, after my holiday, I suspect I'll run into the opposite problem – Iris is a chatterer and has excellent conversational English, and may find Lindsey is not enough for her.

In the Romanian classes, the first and last are perfectly lovely, but the middle one – three teenage boys – is not. I nag, cajole, and threaten. I use the "Your parents are paying good money for this" line. I use the "Why am I even here?" line. I message the organiser. I talk to myself. I swear internally, and am pleased when it ends. The lesson the normal teacher had left no work for, however, is a joy to teach and makes me consider again whether I should offer an afternoon each week to this company for regular classes. The main thing stopping me is not that is pays half my Chinese hourly rate, but that I suspect it will lack the flexibility my Chinese company and private classes bring. I have become accustomed to finding it easy and painless to ask for time off, and would not wish to relinquish this in any great hurry.

Monday, Tuesday, and Wednesday next week are the Chinese May holidays, so I have very few classes on those days. It's rare that a Chinese holiday coincides with a bank holiday in Ireland. I'm ridiculously happy at the thought of days off.

May

Monday 1st May 2023
Number of classes: 0
Number of students: 0
Lessons to plan for tomorrow: 0

The zeros suggest I am not working today. This is because I am not working today. But I still find a string of angry messages and emails from Dorrie's mum wanting to know why I am not there to speak to Dorrie, despite the fact that I did not schedule a class and told Dorrie quite clearly that we have no lesson today due to the holiday. Aside from this, my husband and I were busy burying out cat at the time I would usually have this class, so I was not impressed by this tirade and am more certain than ever that my days on this platform are heading fast towards *Over*.

TUESDAY 2ND MAY 2023
NUMBER OF CLASSES: 1
NUMBER OF STUDENTS: 1
LESSONS TO PLAN FOR TOMORROW: 1

I meet only Dorrie today, and I only kept her scheduled to ensure I get up and don't waste the day with an extra-long lie-in.

WEDNESDAY 3RD MAY 2023
NUMBER OF CLASSES: 2
NUMBER OF STUDENTS: 1+2
LESSONS TO PLAN FOR TOMORROW: 1

I wake to a message asking if I could do emergency cover for the same teacher I covered Romanian classes for on Friday. I am almost tempted, but it feels a lot like it would defeat the thrill of having most of the day off, so I turn it down.

Whilst my company classes are still on holiday, Harry and Susie choose to go ahead with theirs so I spend the time I'd usually be teaching the literature classes for the company preparing a *George's Marvellous Medicine* lesson. It doesn't take long.

Susie and Harry invent their own marvellous medicines in the class today. Susie's will allow the drinker to fly. Harry's will kill. I know whose I'll be more inclined to sample.

Language Linkers, a charity I sometimes volunteer for, have emailed to say they need volunteers (or possibly paid tutors) to facilitate a project with Afghan refugees who are stuck in limbo in Pakistan awaiting transfer to the UK. It sounds interesting and I submit my interest.

Thursday 4th May 2023
Number of classes: 3
Number of students: 4+3+?
Lessons to plan for tomorrow: 0

In the first class of the day, we are writing biographies. Evelyn has come prepared with a book about Walt Disney – a great choice! Luna has chosen a basketball player I haven't heard of, and whom she needs to research. She'll use her iPad, she decides. Kim wants to write about his dad. "Is he interesting?" I ask. Kim can't answer that, so I ask why he has chosen his dad. I can't argue with his logic when he explains that he knows his dad really well – everything about him (really???) – so he'll be able to write well about him. However, we watch a video about Katherine Johnson, and Kim amazes me with his knowledge of racial segregation and an awareness that women were not equal either in 1960s America, and he immediately decides to write about this instead. This new, attentive, hard-working, engaged Kim is not the Kim I taught in his previous class, and I like him so much better for it.

I have another day off tomorrow, so it's a lovely relaxing week all round! I should have had a class with Lindsey, but as the company class is having a week's break between courses, I have cancelled Lindsey too. These are the true perks of having left the big companies after the collapse of much of the Chinese ESL market a couple of years ago.

Monday 8th May 2023
Number of classes: 4
Number of students: 1+3+4+1
Lessons to plan for tomorrow: 2

How lovely it was to have a long weekend and most of last week off! The flip side of that is that I already have no idea which day it is, and it's hard to get back into the swing of work.

A new trial student joins Apple and Sky today, which I'm not delighted about, as those two work so well together I'm worried a new student will upset their balance. As it turns out, the new student is pretty good, but has horrendous feedback noise on her device, so the class is hard work regardless of student behaviour or ability and I'm not sorry when it ends. If she comes back next week, she'd better have sorted her sound out. Classes with excessive background noise or feedback are mentally and physically draining. I always have to speak a lot more in these classes, and louder, too, and feel like I've run up a very steep hill by the time I'm done.

My beginner, Yiyi, is coming on very well. Her little sister doesn't participate much, but her mum makes up for that in spades. I'll have to gently nudge her out soon. While background noise and feedback is probably the biggest problem in online teaching, interfering parents comes a close second. Having a parent repeat everything, and correct their child, and interrupt the class constantly to do both is extremely annoying. And unhelpful.

This afternoon, I manage to not only plan both of the lessons I needed to make for tomorrow, but also one of Wednesday's three too. Wednesdays are my best day in terms of students and lessons – all three classes are literature-based, which I much prefer – but in terms of preparation, it's the worst day as each of those lessons needs making almost from scratch and takes forever to do.

Tuesday 9th May 2023
Number of classes: 4
Number of students: 1+2+4+2
Lessons to plan for tomorrow: 2

Kayley does better in her lesson today — finally! Her whole class group is coming on very well from having added that easier course to reinforce their GK learning before making the leap to G1. I appreciate this company more than I could have ever imagined when I started working for them. Past companies would never have created an extra bridging lesson, or done anything that could be interpreted as taking a step backwards in order to take the children forwards.

I just wish that Catherine's mum had listened to me too, when I told her *Wonder* was too much of a jump for Catherine and Mango. I have a LOT of teacher-talk time in these classes now. I'm having to explain large chunks of the text each lesson, and I can't tell whether it's because they don't really understand the book, or whether it's because they simply can't remember what they have read. I know Catherine already read to the end within the first couple of lessons, so asking her to then recall information from the middle of the book for the chapters we are discussing is hard. Meanwhile I think Mango has found it hard-going generally. I have no doubt that both girls can READ the words, but a whole lot of doubt that they have full comprehension of huge parts of the book. I'm bored with it, and I can't imagine they aren't. I will never understand this desire to push ESL students into work that is far too hard. They become much more confidently fluent from general chat and discussing things they are comfortable with, rather than struggling to dissect meaning before they can even try to form an answer. I can't wait to finish this book.

Wednesday 10th May 2023
Number of classes: 3
Number of students: 4+3+2
Lessons to plan for tomorrow: 1

My favourite day for teaching!

Each class runs smoothly and well. We run out of time in the second and third, but in the third it doesn't matter because we will just continue from where we got to next time and I will have less planning to do too. In the other, it's not really important either – we spent about thirty minutes writing a poem and didn't have time to discuss our feelings about poetry

DON'T SQUEEZE THE TURTLE

or watch a video about similes, but hey, we wrote a damn fine poem! Here it is:

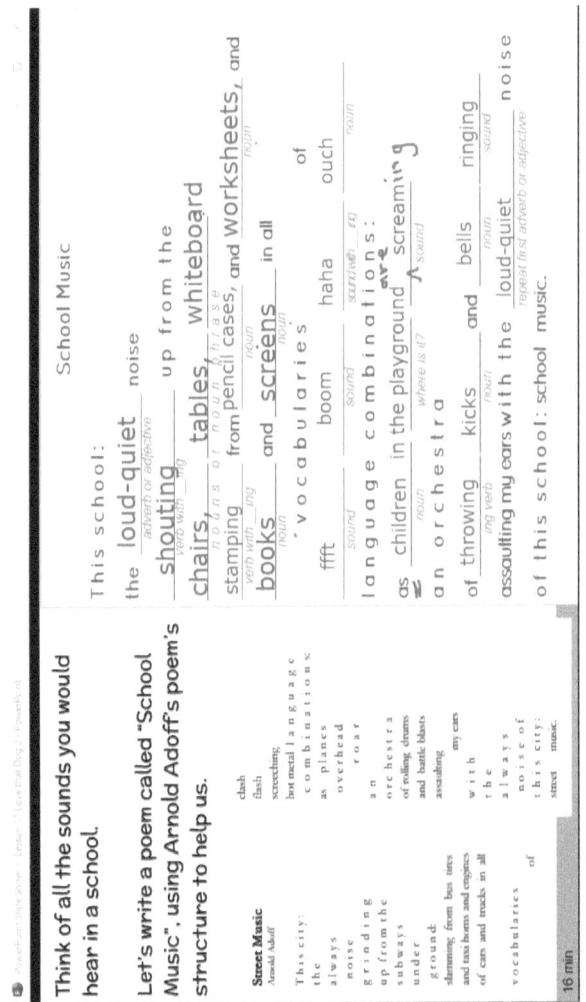

School Music, by Natalie, Honey, and Sophia

What more can I ask for? (Actually, possibly for Honey and Natalie to have contributed a bit more rather than Sophia doing the bulk of it, but ...)

I wish all my classes were like Wednesday classes, except without the preparation.

In good news, I also have no more prep to do for the rest of this week, having done both the lesson for tomorrow and the Friday lesson before I write this diary entry.

Thursday 11th May 2023
Number of classes: 3
Number of students: 4+2+3
Lessons to plan for tomorrow: 0

In the first class, Teresa tells me she has still not spoken to her grandfather, which leaves her still unable to begin her biography. Kim, meanwhile, has fully embraced writing about Katherine Johnson and shares heaps of facts, but also asks a lot of questions. Luckily, oh so luckily, Luna and Evelyn both know exactly what they want to get on with, and do so, working independently for almost the entire class. I juggle helping Teresa plan with helping Kim answer research questions, which is fine until Teresa loses her sound and can no longer hear me. This means toggling between Googled information about Katherine Johnson on one screen while writing Teresa instructions, questions, and ideas on the whiteboard on the second screen. It turns out her grandfather is a famous Chinese actor, but her mum won't let her tell us who. Jackie Chan? If it's not him, I won't have heard of him anyway.

Kevin and Craig have an equally un-smooth lesson, where the aim is to revise verbs, but the result is a whole lot of mistyped words, annotations that don't work properly, and a freewrite involving spaghetti. We do, at least, laugh a lot.

Cynthia, just when I thought the day's class couldn't get any more chaotic, wears a blue origami box on her head for the entire lesson, and a white one on top of that for part of the lesson, and, once again, puts her poor mum on camera so I can "ask her, then". Today, the question Cynthia wants me to ask her mother is, "Do you help your mum." Cynthia says no, shoves the camera into her mum's face, and her mum says, "A little bit." My money's on Cynthia's answer being the more accurate.

Friday 12th May 2023
Number of classes: 2
Number of students: 1+4
Lessons to plan for Monday: 1

Lindsey and I have a useful one-to-one class, but I am a little worried that she won't be a good match for Iris, as her conversational skills are significantly lower than Iris's. I hope that Lindsey will be encouraged to stretch herself, rather than dispirited by the new match, and that Iris will be patient with her. I haven't yet told Lindsey's parents that I want the girls to study *George's Marvellous Medicine*, and I only have another two weeks to prepare Lindsey for that jump.

In my company class, Eric falls asleep. There's always one in this class, but it's usually Sean. It's so late for these young boys to be studying, especially on a Friday at the end of a long week.

Monday 15th May 2023
Number of classes: 4
Number of students: 1+2+4+1
Lessons to plan for tomorrow: 1

Sky and Apple are not on their usual sparkling form today – Sky has some problems with his iPad – and does that thing where he logs in from two devices simultaneously and explodes my ears – and is distracted in trying to fix that for most of the class, while I battle with hearing anything other than my own voice in the feedback. Apple spends half the class asking me what I've said instead of listening while I say it. Not their best effort.

Rain slips further and further behind as he now has three classmates who are at a level above his and cope well with the work. He tries his best, but understands little and tries to answer questions by finding some random part of the book to read to me.

Which he also can't do.

He has good understanding of the stories, and WANTS to communicate his ideas, but he hasn't the vocabulary or communication skills to either fully understand what he's being asked, or to answer accurately. It's a shame he's not with children of his level as it would help him a lot.

Catherine and Mango have cancelled tomorrow's class – Mango is sick, maybe with Covid. I am in the middle of prepping their lesson when the message arrives, so finish the prep anyway. One less to prepare next week. That their class is cancelled tomorrow is a help in terms of time to prepare Wednesday's lessons, too; I'll use that spare hour to get them done.

TUESDAY 16TH MAY 2023
NUMBER OF CLASSES: 3
NUMBER OF STUDENTS: 1+2+4
LESSONS TO PLAN FOR TOMORROW: 3

It is Kate's mum's birthday tomorrow but her dad is in China and wants to drink beer with his friends, so he's just flying to Hong Kong today to do dating with Kate's mum and eat cake and then he's going back to China for the beer. Happy birthday Kate's mum, he sounds like a keeper!

WEDNESDAY 17TH MAY 2023
NUMBER OF CLASSES: 3
NUMBER OF STUDENTS: 3+3+2
LESSONS TO PLAN FOR TOMORROW: 1

Genuinely nothing exciting or memorable happens in classes today. Susie has her same old internet trouble to start with, but she fixes it and manages to stay in class, on camera, with working audio, for the duration. I suppose that, in itself, is noteworthy.

THURSDAY 18TH MAY 2023
NUMBER OF CLASSES: 3
NUMBER OF STUDENTS: 4+3+4
LESSONS TO PLAN FOR TOMORROW: 1

Is there anything so lovely as a student eating a mouthful of rice, close-up to the camera, in a great lump, which she chews open-mouthed and lets fall back into her bowl? I am currently camera-off waiting for the class to start. I could turn her camera off, but then she will realise I'm here, and I don't want her to know I'm here because then she will also want to talk to me, whilst still chewing/spilling food from her mouth.

In Kevin's class, he is so busy reading *Diary of a Wimpy Kid*[1] that he pays little attention to anything else until it is time to stop thinking about adjectives and adverbs and other tedious grammar rules, and begin to write. Then, he leaps into action and writes yet another story in which I die a slow and painful death. Craig, unsurprisingly, also makes me the main character of his story, but although there is much violence, and some questionable cliff-hanging moments where I wonder if I will survive, I not only live, but go on to be awarded a Nobel prize for my efforts. I'm not entirely sure what the efforts were, unless it was a determined effort to not succumb to the attack of the broken, but still sharp, pencil that featured in the story.

In the final class, Luffy tells us things haven't gone well for him today. His Pumpkin UFO (the one he uses most weeks to get to school) broke when he visited space earlier this morning. He has a pair of pliers though, so is confident he can fix it before bedtime. He'd better work fast – their class only finishes at 9 p.m. Beijing time, so I doubt there's much time before bed.

---

1. Kinney, J, *Diary of a Wimpy Kid*, Puffin Books, 2007

Friday 19th May 2023
Number of classes: 2
Number of students: 1+3
Lessons to plan for Monday: 1

I task Lindsey with quite a lot of writing today, to prepare for the lessons with Iris, but she needs more help than I expected. She has written independently in past classes, but not for a while. I do hope the new pairing will work out.

In the company class, Bourne is absent, and no one falls asleep, so that felt like a win. Jerry is getting more chatty now too, so this is an easier class than most Fridays bring.

Monday 22nd May 2023
Number of classes: 3
Number of students: 1+4+4+1
Lessons to plan for tomorrow: 1

Jessica is back today, with her arm in a cast and sling, and a bandage around her leg, but I can't decipher what had happened to her.

Yiyi is making lovely progress, but I barely see Xiaorou, so it lurks in my mind that their mum will question the cost of the class if it's just the one child: it will be the same.

Tuesday 23rd May 2023
Number of classes: 3 (4?)
Number of students: 1+0+4+2
Lessons to plan for tomorrow: 3

I know my ESL colleagues would be incensed by a last minute cancellation, but how I love them! I am just entering the Zoom room for the first company class when I get a message to say Honey isn't coming – poor Honey is so over-worked. I had already had a message to say she hadn't had time to do her homework, which is not unusual, but then as I enter the class, another message to say she is too tired to come today. Kate, unusually, isn't waiting for me in the classroom. It turns out she is sick too, so I am quick to suggest a postponement. I have heaps to do – Tuesday is my biggest prep day, so if I can clear at least one lesson in this free hour, it will be a bonus.

Kayley, once again, holds her classmates back beyond sanity with her inability to copy even a simple sentence accurately while her classmates extend and expand and turn their four-word sentence into an entire short story while I limp through writing **We have ten hens**. with Kayley. I'm not often stumped, but I have no idea how to get through to this girl. In another example, despite my writing the correct version on the screen, writing it on my physical whiteboard to model, getting all three other students to show their correct work, and talking through step by painful step, Kayley can not amend **did ben go to school**. She can neither capitalise the **b** in **ben**, nor add the question mark. In the end, Eric defaults to her level and stops speaking or sharing his work, while I dismiss Apple and Jolin from the class a few minutes early to silently scream at the other two while outwardly trying to help them. Apple and Jolin both write epic sagas about those bloody hens.

Wednesday 24th May 2023
Number of classes: 3
Number of students: 4+3+2
Lessons to plan for tomorrow: 1

Poor Honey. It is as I expected – she is overwhelmed by how much work she has each week. She is cheerful, and has good news to share for once, but is tired and overworked. Even though she missed yesterday's class, she still hasn't had time to finish reading our relatively short narrative poem novel, *Hate that Cat*[2], and I already know that even with a two-week gap while I am on holiday, she won't read all of our next, longer, novel. I've only asked them to read the first two or three chapters, but my money says she won't even manage that.

Susie has the same old same old tech issues, which is very tiresome. I wonder if her parents will decide it's more hassle than it's worth to try to do online classes, however nice it is to have her back in class.

THURSDAY 25TH MAY 2023
NUMBER OF CLASSES: 3
NUMBER OF STUDENTS: 3+3+4
LESSONS TO PLAN FOR TOMORROW: 0

Teresa hasn't written any of her grandfather's biography, still. She has, at least, done a bit more research, in that she asked her grandmother some questions, and she did tell me the name of one of his films in that she asked me how to spell the name of

---

2. Creech, S, *Hate that Cat*, Bloomsbury, 2008

it, but still won't share exactly who her grandfather is. I don't know what she thinks I would do with the information.

I finish every class today with instructions for 'while I'm on holiday' homework, and unconcealed excitement about having three weeks away from their classes.

Friday 26th May 2023
Number of classes: 2
Number of students: 1+4
Lessons to plan for Monday: 1

I've geared Lindsey's mum up for starting class with Iris after I get home from my holiday, although I have increasing reservations about whether the girls will match well. Lindsey needs a lot more help with her writing than I had anticipated, and Iris will be streets ahead. We'll give it a try, and I've sent Lindsey's mum my "here's what I plan to do" PPT for the first *George's Marvellous Medicine* lesson and a PDF of the entire book. She's not said much yet.

In the second class, I go through the same "I'm going on holiday" spiel, but this turns into a lengthy show-and-tell with a calendar, so Eric can understand whether he was having his

Tuesday lessons as normal or whether I am only away for the three Fridays, but popping home to teach him on Tuesdays.

MONDAY 29TH MAY 2023
NUMBER OF CLASSES: 4
NUMBER OF STUDENTS: 1+4+4+1
LESSONS TO PLAN FOR TOMORROW: 2

I've forgotten to scan the next part of *Harry Potter* for Dorrie, so tell her we will read to the end of the chapter (less than a page and a half) and then not start the new chapter until after my holiday, to avoid leaving a chapter partway through. Ten minutes into the lesson time, five of which we spent chatting, we have finished the chapter, and I'm frantically scanning the next one onto the screen as we go. We won't finish it before I go on holiday, so will leave the chapter hanging partway through after all. So much for plans.

My quiet Monday company classes with two students each have both filled to four students in both, but Rain excels today, in that neither Xika nor Winson had read the text ahead of class, so Rain and Belle have to summarise for them. Rain does well to tell a good part of the story. We spend more of the class discussing what a hijab is than talking about the actual story, which is a nice aside.

I keep forgetting I have TWO classes to prep for Tuesday. I'm *very* bored of *Wonder* now, and running out of 'making it interesting' lessons.

Tuesday 30th May 2023
Number of classes: 4
Number of students: 1+2+4+2
Lessons to plan for tomorrow: 3

I'm on a definite wind-down for my holiday now and mention *many* times in each lesson that I'm off on my hols. Most of my students now know where the Baltic Sea is, and which countries I'll be visiting. It's like a geography lesson free with every class, this week.

Dorrie and I have, as predicted, abandoned a *Harry Potter* chapter midway through, and I also predict we'll just start that chapter over when I get back.

Honey was reluctant to come to class again today. She has become so stressed with how much work she has to do – she has exams this week too – but she is also a worrier and panics that she is behind with the work. Because of this, I adapt today's lesson – both girls have finished working on their non-fiction projects anyway, so I decided to improvise and let the girls choose what they want to write. Kate chooses to write about the seasons, and Honey writes some acrostic poems, using her inspiration from our Wednesday Literature class, and the book we've been reading there: *Love that Dog*. These girls love writing and are both very creative; they both share stories they'd written outside this class, and the relaxed lesson we have today hopefully goes some way to reminding them this is meant to be something they enjoy doing, not a chore they dread.

In the other of my company classes, Kayley is on good form today, and this class is easier than often. Apple, as usual, wants to cram in an encyclopaedia-worth of information into every part of her writing, and her caption for her polar bear picture threatens to spill over her pages. Their pictures, on the whole, are as bad as mine. Polar bears are not an easy animal to draw, even with a picture in front of us to copy.

With Catherine and Mango, *Wonder* is not getting any more fun. It has taken us six months and we still have two-and-a-bit sections to get through.

WEDNESDAY 31ST MAY 2023
NUMBER OF CLASSES: 3
NUMBER OF STUDENTS: 3+3+2
LESSONS TO PLAN FOR TOMORROW: 0 AND 0 FOR THE NEXT TWO-AND-A-HALF WEEKS! YAY!

In the G3 Literature class, we start our new text, *Number the Stars*.[3] It's a wartime story of Jewish oppression and holocaust, with heavy, heavy themes. The girls have the English skills to read the book easily, but they lack the background knowledge to fully comprehend the information in the story. With a LOT of preparation done yesterday, we use most of today's lesson to do a whistle-stop learning of WWII, concentration camps, and ethnic cleansing, so that makes for cheerful content. While preparing the work, I realised that I'll be visiting some of the places we read about, so I promise to try to get pictures of the streets or places named in the book.

I finish the morning with Harry, Susie, and George Kranky, then pack up my teaching head and throw together the rest of the packing. Did I mention we're off on holiday tomorrow?

---

3. Lowry, L, *Number the Stars*, Harper Collins, 1990

June

Monday 19th June 2023
Number of classes: 3
Number of students: 4+4+2
Lessons to plan for tomorrow: 2

It's weirdly nice to back to the classrooms today, although I'd be happy enough to take the rest of the week off now one day is done. Dorrie is off this week for Dragon Boat Festival, so I am eased back into work with a gentle start, and a break after the first class to boot. Classes run surprisingly smoothly:

- Jessica has the cast off her arm

- Sky corrects my English a couple of times

- Only one student is late

- Xiaorou says hello before going off to bed.

That's the level of the day's work, but now I've loads of preparation for the week looming to keep me busy for the foreseeable future and I'd rather do a million other things instead.

Tuesday 20th June 2023
Number of classes: 3
Number of students: 2+3+2
Lessons to plan for tomorrow: 3

It's not very nice of me to feel relieved that I wake to a message saying Kayley will be absent from class today, but it will make her class so much easier and more enjoyable. Now if only Eric has learned to write faster during my holiday, that would be the icing on the cake.

I'm writing this while Kate and Honey are quietly writing for the last ten-fifteen minutes of their class. Kate is writing a brief introduction to cars, and Honey, ever-short on thinking of ideas quickly, and always dismissive of my suggestions, is writing about her brother again. Their only criteria today is that their writing must be non-fiction. We've had a lovely class casually chatting about where I went on holiday and what they got up to while I was gone (nothing much), and skimming through a non-fiction book about how to read non-fiction books, which amused Honey a lot. We wonder if the non-fiction book the non-fiction book was telling us how to read was also about a non-fiction book.

The main topic of today's three short in-class videos is the importance of a good introduction and a good strong closing. After writing for ten minutes, Kate stops to ask if she needs to include either, and I realise the point of the videos was entirely missed.

In the next class – the one without Kayley – the task is to write a fantasy story, and this is *infinitely* easier with just the three students. Eric, as usual, has great ideas, but when he shows me his writing, I have no idea what it is supposed to say, as his written English is still very much at the 'Emergent' level:

The dragon is litagud.

Luckily, he remembers his intentions, and when I ask him to read it to me, it comes out as "The dragon is little and cute." Aw, cute. (Or, *Aw, litagud*.)

Wednesday 21st June 2023
Number of classes: 3
Number of students: 2+2+2
Lessons to plan for tomorrow: 1

Lesson 1: Spring's camera is on but she's not there. A message tells me Bruno will be late – he always is, so that's no surprise. Belle, apparently, has quit the class. Why? I ask. She thinks it's too easy for her. To be fair, I thought it would be, but she hasn't really shown that it is, so I'm surprised to hear this. Bruno shows up about twenty minutes in, and Spring enjoys a bit of useful one-to-one.

Lesson 2: A student who I think is Honey is in class, in that her Zoom is connected but her camera and audio are off. The name is in Chinese, but I think I recognise it as Honey's Chinese name. I call hello into the void a few times before realising that my own camera and mic are also off, so the mystery student can't hear me trying to identify her. Meanwhile, I know it's not Natalie as I get a message just as the class starts to say she'll be absent. Honey and I turn on our cameras and mics and Honey, like Spring in the previous class, also enjoys some useful one-to-one. We go over some more background of WWII and the Holocaust for twenty minutes or so until Sophia rolls up.

Lesson 3: Susie is ready and waiting. I message Harry three times to prompt him to come to class while making idle chat with Susie. Susie enjoys some internet-stable one-to-one for about twenty minutes before Harry turns up.

I still like Wednesdays best, though. And there's always benefit in one-to-one time.

THURSDAY 22ND JUNE 2023
NUMBER OF CLASSES: 3 2
NUMBER OF STUDENTS: 4 2 + 4 0 + 4 3
LESSONS TO PLAN FOR TOMORROW: 1

I wake to this message at 8.17 A.M.:
Fiona: *lots of students asks for a leave*
I reply: I *think it is a holiday in China this week?*
Fiona: *yes. from today*
Fiona: *last for 3 days*
I reply: *We can postpone classes until next week if they prefer*
Fiona: *we will send video to them*
Fiona: *pls teach as usual*

Ok, I answer, and get up. I wouldn't have minded a day off. Even though I just had three weeks off in the Baltics.

At 10.51 A.M., just as I'm about to start the first class, this pops into my inbox:
Alice asks for a leave
Alice has yet to attend this class, so I'm hardly surprised, but this message is followed immediately by: *Let's postpone the 7pm class. All the students can't attend it*

Meanwhile, the class I'm about to start is about to start, and this message arrives: *Teresa asks for a leave (6pm)*
OK, no problem, I answer, because it's really not. I'm happy teaching as few students as possible anytime! Which is good, because:
Fiona: *Minnie asks for a leave.*

By the end of the morning, I've taught two out of three classes, to five out of twelve students, and had a remarkably peaceful morning.

FRIDAY 23RD JUNE 2023
NUMBER OF CLASSES: 1
NUMBER OF STUDENTS: 3
LESSONS TO PLAN FOR MONDAY: 1

Iris and Lindsey are not starting classes until next week now, so I have just one class today, right in the middle of my day, from 1 P.M. to 2 P.M. It's calm and easy and I learn how to say *Happy Dragon Boat Festival* well enough in Chinese for Jerry, Bourne and Eric to be impressed rather than laugh at me.

MONDAY 26TH JUNE 2023
NUMBER OF CLASSES: 4
NUMBER OF STUDENTS: 1+4+4+2
LESSONS TO PLAN FOR TOMORROW: 2

Me to Yiyi: "How are you today?"
Yiyi: "I am happy." *yawns a huge yawn.
Me: "Are you tired?"
Yiyi: "I am tired."
Xiaorou yawns.
Me: "Is Xiaorou tired?"
Yiyi: "Xiaorou is happy."

Me: *yawns.

Yiyi was, in fact, very tired, and I imagine was asleep within seconds of the class end.

Tuesday 27th June 2023
Number of classes: 4
Number of students: 1+2+4+2
Lessons to plan for tomorrow: 3
Lessons I actually get planned for tomorrow by the end of this long day: 2. Dammit. Now I will have to get up early to do the lesson plan for *Number the Stars*.

On the plus side, Catherine and Mango have nearly finished *Wonder*, and are away next week so I won't have to teach it for a while. In an ideal world I will plan the lesson anyway, so I am ahead of myself for once, but I won't be doing it today.

Wednesday 28th June 2023
Number of classes: 3
Number of students: 2+3+2
Lessons to plan for tomorrow: 0

Only Spring and Bruno now attend the first of today's classes, and it's doing them good to have to work harder without Belle to help. Bruno is in his car waiting to take part in a cart race, so in the break, he takes us on a tour of the trackside. He is the youngest competitor, he says, and many of the other racers are adults.

Natalie is only up to Chapter 4 of *Number the Stars*, and has not watched the class recording from last time, so we have to try to cram a lot of the background information from last week into this week. It is Honey's birthday, and not only did she have a huge final test at school, but she then has to discuss the horrors of the holocaust in great detail. I hope she gets a lovely cake to compensate!

Thursday 29th June 2023
Number of classes: 3
Number of students: 4+2+4
Lessons to plan for tomorrow: 0

I get a message to say Alice asks for a leave. Alice still has not attended this class and we are six lessons in. Craig, apparently, is in America and will also be absent. I'm sure he didn't mention he was going, although he often talks about America. I think he lived there before. The class should be easy with only Kevin and Orlando, but Orlando has some unidentifiable tech issue that only his family are aware of – I can hear and see him fine, and there is no lagging, but his mother hovers over him messing with his iPad until eventually he turns off the camera and I don't know if he's there or not. Kevin is in tedious form and is reading a comic instead of paying attention. I don't blame him: this lesson is jam-packed with far too many different grammar and writing points and we have no time left to write a thing. I skip the second half of the lesson, not through choice, but for trying to get them to actually understand the first two points:

1. **Adding detail to weak sentences.** They usually write in great detail and are good at the whole 'show don't tell' thing, but here, they find it difficult and

either change the meaning of the sample sentences, or add an entire essay of extra sentences but leave the original weak sentence as it was.

2. **Compound sentences**. Easier, but drawn-out.

The third point was to focus on complex sentences, but how insane to lump this straight on top of compound sentences and expect them to remember both. It's a good call to skip it.

Friday 30th June 2023
Number of classes: 2
Number of students: 2+4
Lessons to plan for Monday: 1

Iris and Lindsey are due to meet today. Iris's mum has been messaging me since I woke up to tell me all kinds of things she's already told me – mainly about how Iris is a brilliant reader and everything is very easy, but she refuses to recite. I think she means 'write'. I suspect she may also lack some comprehension of what she is reading, but we'll soon find out.

Later:

It's great to see Iris, but she is a few minutes late, and in her car, with chatty mum in the background. She soon arrives home, and Iris's mum proceeds to swap Iris's devices back and forth about six times, which is not a little disruptive! I'll need to rein her in asap and get her to stay out of the classroom if Iris is to have any fun at all in class.

July

Monday 3 July 2023
Number of classes: 4
Number of students: 1+4+4+2
Lessons to plan for tomorrow: 1

Sky, Apple, and Jessica work together to do the vocabulary section, and take turns to read and make their own sentences. The addition of Jessica and Sherry to this class has changed the dynamics significantly and Apple and Sky no longer banter like they used to, but the new girls are competent and sweet and the change is not all bad. Sherry is about fifteen minutes late, because why would I have a class where everyone arrives on time?

In the next class, Xika gives us the point of view of the lollipop from our current story.[1] No one wants to be licked

---

1. Kahn, R, *Big Red Lollipop*, Penguin, 2010

in class, so it's a good thing it's online. I forget the weird time-keeping of this class (Monday classes run to strange times and this one starts at ten past the hour) and accidentally finish ten minutes early. In a previous life as an ESL teacher in a big ESL company, this would have cost me a fine and a warning and a loss of class pay. In this new company, it gets a virtual shrug of understanding.

TUESDAY 4TH JULY 2023
NUMBER OF CLASSES: 3
NUMBER OF STUDENTS: 1+2+4
LESSONS TO PLAN FOR TOMORROW: 3

I tell Kayley's class that I have new hens. Kayley says she loves to eat chicken. And chicken goujons. I am most impressed by her use of 'goujons' but I won't tell the hens what she said.

Wednesday 5th July 2023
Number of classes: 3
Number of students: 2+3+2
Lessons to plan for tomorrow: 1

Honey starts the class today by informing me she thought she was dead.

Last week was her ninth birthday and she's already done? I gently probe for more information, trying to find out what she means, and she disappears for a moment, to returns with a handful of pills – I think three different ones.

I ask if they are medicine or vitamins. She thinks not vitamins. I ask her why her mum had given them to her, and she isn't able to tell me. I wonder if they are to help her relax and be less stressed. She repeats that when she took them, she thought she was dead.

This is one of the strangest conversations I've had in five years of ESL, and leaves me feeling increasingly concerned for Honey.

Thursday 6th July 2023
Number of classes: 3
Number of students: 2+3+2
Lessons to plan for tomorrow: 0

Three of our upstairs windows are being replaced today, with the agreement that I need to use my office from 11 to 2. By 10.50 A.M., they are still banging and crashing around in my office, so I grab my equipment and decamp to the lounge, already under some pressure due to noise, headache, and not having time to get properly organised. I get into the first class at about three minutes to eleven and am greeted (still camera and mic off, catching my breath) by Luna's mum trying to speak to me. Luna, it seems, is off on holiday next week. This happens, especially in summer. None of the other parents feel the need to discuss it with me in great depth.

In the second class, none of the students arrive on time. Kevin is first, at about five minutes late. Alice, unsurprisingly, is not coming. Nimo[2], I guess, is still away. Orlando comes in and out and in and out at about ten past. Kevin, meanwhile, refuses to participate until a classmate shows up, even if he has

---

2. Nimo is Craig. He was called Nimo for the first year or so I taught him, and then changed to a more 'grown-up' name. We use his two names fairly interchangeably in classes, although this is the first time I've noticed having used 'Nimo' in this diary.

to wait for 2000 years. He used to enjoy the lessons a lot more than he seems to now. He has lost his writer's notebook, along with his will for the class.

FRIDAY 7TH JULY 2023
NUMBER OF CLASSES: 2
NUMBER OF STUDENTS: 2+4
LESSONS TO PLAN FOR MONDAY: 1

Iris and Lindsey are fab in their class and produce excellent writing, but I do suspect Iris's mother will be a bit *constant*.

All these Chinese children are under so much pressure to perform and do well. It's supposed to be the summer holidays and they are all still going to classes.

In the second class today, we establish that none of us want Sean to train our dogs. He suggests that a guide dog should learn how to fight with other dogs, run fast across roads, and bite its owner. Great use of vocabulary though, for a four-year-old.

Monday 10th July 2023
Number of classes: 4
Number of students: 1+4+2+1
Lessons to plan for tomorrow: 2

Dorrie's mum messages to let me know she will be on holiday next week, which is handy, as I was going to cancel her anyway while I'm away in England for my Graduation. I love it when it's this easy.

The last few weeks have been stressful overall, due to a difficult houseguest, and severe lack of sleep or downtime. I'm sleepwalking through classes and hoping not to make the same mistake today as last Monday, where I ended the second company class ten minute early.

As it turns out, only two of that class show up, which makes it easier to teach – Rain does better when there are fewer students and I can meet his pace. He astounds me today. He hasn't read the book – he'd read the wrong one instead – but the class begins with a video reading of the book anyway. He takes it in so well, he's able to answer all the questions about story elements and give great detail. Not bad for a child who has very low-level English.

Tuesday 11th July 2023
Number of classes: 4
Number of students: 1+2+4+2
Lessons to plan for tomorrow: 3

Kayley, thank goodness, has turned a corner. She seems to have grasped the idea of writing a sentence! This is probably the most exciting progress any child has made for ages. We are largely discussing our favourite desserts, and she, like me, can't choose – she loves them all. I'm on her side over this topic, which probably endears her to me somewhat.

Wednesday 12th July 2023
Number of classes: 3
Number of students: 2+3+2
Lessons to plan for tomorrow: 1

Natalie takes class from a picnic table on the banks of the River Thames. I offer to meet her in London on Sunday, when I will happen to be there, but her father says they will have moved on to Exeter by then. I have tried to send my email address to him, as he requested, but I'm not certain it will get passed on – this is usually against ESL company policy to stop teachers poaching students for private lessons.

I've given in to my better judgement and asked for Monday off, alongside my already-booked Tuesday. Everyone agrees easily and willingly, which *should* have taken a weight off me for my travel plans next week. The ease was momentary, as the floor fitter calls to say he will fit our new floor on Monday. We leave for England on Saturday and must now clear out the entire contents of the living room before we go.

THURSDAY 13TH JULY 2023
NUMBER OF CLASSES: 3
NUMBER OF STUDENTS: 1+3+2
LESSONS TO PLAN FOR TOMORROW: 0

Holiday season gives me a one-to-one class with Kim, and where a few months ago, this would have been a tedious exercise in talking to myself, he is engaged and fun and we brainstorm ways to improve his story by adding detail. He self-corrects his irregular verbs and I bask in the smug glow of teaching a boy who has *improved*.

The lessons for the second class have taken a bit of a turn. Last week, and the previous six, were loaded to the brim with grammar practice. Usually several different grammar points jammed into each lesson. We haven't had time to do any free-writing, or even any guided writing. Today's lesson has reverted to the more usual type of writing course lesson, with few slides and much for me to add or improvise. I hope this is here to stay. I wonder if it's a result of my moan last week about how impossible the new lessons were.

Friday 14th July 2023
Number of classes: 2
Number of students: 2+3
Lessons to plan for Monday: 0 because i have the day off.
Lessons to plan for Wednesday: 3

Iris begins the lesson in her car, late, again, with her mother talking in the background and answering for her. She loses connection as she leaves the car, and then is too impatient to wait for me to admit her to the class from the waiting room, so leaves before I can admit her each time. I then get stroppy messages on WeChat (which I don't see till later, because, you know, I'm busy trying to teach a class). When Iris is finally ready to join the class properly, Lindsey and I are halfway through the lesson. I adore Iris, but until we reconnected over the last few weeks, I had wiped from memory how much hard work her mum is.

Tuesday 18th July
Number of classes: 0
Number of students: 0
Number of students texting me to ask is there class today: 2

I am at my MA Graduation today. Catherine and Mango have forgotten and both arrive in class. I don't see this until after the ceremony, and neither of them respond to my message or photo reminding them why I am not in class today.

Wednesday 19th July 2023
Number of classes: 3
Number of students: 2+3+2
Lessons to plan for tomorrow: 1

Natalie is still in the UK. I know this because she has sent me some great photos of London and a letter. I flew into London on Saturday evening, but her family left London on Saturday afternoon, to head south as I headed north. So near yet so far. I've yet to meet any of my students in real life and this is the closest it's got. As she is still travelling, she's not in class today. Without her, Honey and Sophia and I finish *Number the Stars*, and once again, I fight back tears as I read part of it aloud. I'm glad it's over, although it is a great book to teach.

Harry and Susie are prepping for PET tests, so I've had to do a lot of research and resource-gathering. It seems impossible to buy the handbooks, although easy to download them. I would prefer to have an actual book to refer to – it's so hard to read from screen all the time, and impossible to annotate or mark pages. I'm teetering on the edge of printing a several-hundred-page manual.

Thursday 20th July 2023
Number of classes: 3
Number of students: 2+2+4
Lessons to plan for tomorrow: 0

Minnie and Teresa are absent again. Kim and Luna are trying to work on rhyming couplets but although they can think of rhyming words quite easily, they can't make them into proper couplets, as they can't quite grasp that the rhyming words need to go at the end of each line. I deliver almost the entire lesson in off-the-cuff rhyming couplets, but it doesn't help.

Friday 21st July
Number of classes: 2
Number of students: 2+2
Lessons to plan for Monday: 1

Some days are like trying to get blood from stones. Some days the children are so tired they just yawn or sleep. No prizes for guessing what happens to me if the students can't stop yawning.

Monday 24th July
Number of classes: 4
Number of students: 1+4+4+1
Number of lessons to plan for tomorrow: 2

Yiyi is surrounded by hangers-on today – she is in her grandmother's house, with an aunt, uncle, and cousin peering at the screen or lounging on the bed behind her. Her mum logs in on a separate device, and she and Yiyi's dad chip in helpfully throughout the class. It would be easier for Yiyi to speak to me if she could get a word in.

Tuesday 25th July
Number of classes: 4
Number of students: 1+2+4+2
Number of lessons to plan for tomorrow: 3

Iris, apparently, having done, what? *three* classes so far? is off to summer camp and will miss the next three weeks. As Susie is also away this week, I message Lindsey's mum to suggest Lindsey joins Harry in his class tomorrow. I hope Harry's mum won't mind! It will be good for both students to meet someone new to practice English with, but more importantly, it means I get an hour free and don't have to teach two full classes for half pay. Win win.

In the next class, Mango, unusually, is absent and doesn't respond to my messages.[3]

WEDNESDAY 26TH JULY
NUMBER OF CLASSES: 3
NUMBER OF STUDENTS: 1+3+2
NUMBER OF LESSONS TO PLAN FOR TOMORROW: 1

Spring is all alone again in class today. This is doing her the world of good, and allowing us to really focus on building her conversational skills. As an easy bonus, today's book is covered in just one lesson, so Bruno won't be playing catch up if he joins us next week. Spring begins their new course today, and once again, we are having to rejig the choice of books to suit the level of students – the books Spring and Bruno will cover in G3 are the same books Natalie, Honey, and Sophia

---

3. Many days after the class, I realise she told me ages ago she would be on holiday today and we were supposed to cancel the class. Oops.

steamed through in G2, and I still think Spring may find some of the longer chapter books beyond her capabilities for now. I'm anticipating throwing the same revised list at the Monday Literature group, too, and already dreading how Rain will keep up with the reading.

Honey, Natalie, and Sophia finish their G3 course today, and we are both pleased and sorry to say goodbye to *Number the Stars*. Natalie is nail-on-head with saying that she didn't exactly enjoy the book but appreciated learning about the Holocaust. (I'm paraphrasing, of course, but that's her gist.) It's *Charlotte's Web*[4] next — we go from the persecution and execution of Jews to a talking pig in the space of a couple of weeks.

Lindsey and Harry meet for the first time in their 'thrown together' lesson. I ask them to say hello, and if they want to ask each other anything.

"No," says Harry.

"No," says Lindsey.

So that's the introductions over.

---

4. White, E.B., *Charlotte's Web*, Puffin, 1963

Thursday 27th July
Number of classes: 4
Number of students: 2/1+1/0+2+1
Number of lessons to plan for Monday: 1

Today brings the first airport class I've had in a while. We sit at the boarding gate in Hong Kong airport – blissfully calm and quiet, bar the odd announcement – then we board Luna's flight to Taiwan. It's not Ryanair, that's for sure. Unfortunately she has to disconnect before take-off, so we don't get the holiday. This kind of disjointed class – background noise, movement, constant distractions – is hard work, and does little to alleviate my headache.

In the second class, no one arrives. Kevin, it transpires, is also travelling today and hasn't yet arrived at his hotel. Orlando, after five minutes, shows up as present, but as has become his norm, has internet trouble. I can't see him or hear him. After a while, he drops out and I'm alone again. I suggest cancelling the class, but then he reappears. Ish. As in, no camera still. He does manage to speak this time, which is weird, as Zoom doesn't show him to have a microphone. But then he's gone again. I get agreement to cancel the class, but Orlando has 'reconnected' on a different device. Or not, as I still can't see or hear him. He is, apparently, also travelling. He is on the high-speed train, which does not have high-speed internet. We cancel the class and I walk the dogs instead.

In the final class, only Luffy and Jenny are here. Cynthia and Jolin are also on holiday – Jolin attended class from the beach in Sanya on Tuesday, but I'm not sorry she is taking a break today. These students work hard and although I like to see the scenery as they travel around on holiday, it always seems a shame that they get little down time.

This afternoon, it's lovely to see Mira again, after a few weeks break.

FRIDAY 28TH JULY
NUMBER OF CLASSES: 2
NUMBER OF STUDENTS: 2+1
NUMBER OF LESSONS TO PLAN FOR MONDAY: 1

With Sean absent from class, the other three boys have to work much harder. Jerry is coming out of his shell and talking a lot more in both his classes, which is progress. Bourne, as always, loses concentration halfway through the lesson, and Eric can't manage to get connected, so I'm not counting him as 'here'. A quick chat with Mira after the boys' class, and that's the end of an easy day.

Monday 31st July
Number of classes: 3
Number of students: 3+4+1
Number of lessons to plan for tomorrow: 2

Dorrie, due to the pressure of preparing for her move to the next school – high school, I guess, as she is almost 14, has dropped her Monday session. I can't pretend to mind! I adore Dorrie and the chat is easy – we are still reading the second *Harry Potter* – but the platform we use has become a nightmare to use since all the changes they made. I've already dropped most of the few classes I was hanging onto and haven't missed it at all.

Jessica, while thinking up effects to follow the cause: ***I am hungry***, comes up with: "I am hungry so I will go to the supermarket and get a tomato." I must look confused, as she then corrects it to the equally unappetising: "I will go to the supermarket and get a potato."

Unless, of course, it's freshly baked and smothered with cheese, in which case, it might do the trick. I am imagining a poor hungry child, clutching a single, slightly grubby, uncooked potato, and taking a bite.

The tomato, on reflection, would have been the better choice, although I suspect she'd still be a bit peckish afterwards.

August

Tueday 1st August
Number of classes: 4
Number of students: 1+1+3+2
Number of lessons to plan for tomorrow: 3

We have so nearly finished *Wonder*!!! We run out of time to write the book review, but by next week I can close this book and be done with it. We have been working on it since January, and although Catherine has coped well, Mango has found it difficult. I, meanwhile, am simply bored to tears with it.

The catch with being almost finished is that now we have to agree on what to do next.

Wednesday 2nd August
Number of classes: 3
Number of students: 2+2+2
Number of lessons to plan for tomorrow: 1

I wake to a message about Honey. Honey hasn't yet responded to say whether she will continue with either of her classes – both her courses restart with new levels this week. Can I write her a message to convince her, I am begged.

I do this, and write a long spiel about how much easier the next couple of books will be, and how much I adore her.

We send it.

I get a message back to say the only reason she hadn't responded or come to class is that she's on holiday. My begging wasn't needed.

Harry and Susie have so many connection problems that our timed 45-minute practice test drags into an extra twenty minutes of class time.

THURSDAY 3 AUGUST
NUMBER OF CLASSES: 4
NUMBER OF STUDENTS: 2+2+4+1
NUMBER OF LESSONS TO PLAN FOR TOMORROW: 0

In Luna and Kim's class, we discuss personification. We practice personification. I give examples of personification. We watch a video of personification. I put a list of objects on screen and tell the students I'll give them five minutes to come up with some ideas of how to personify these things.

"Teacher," Kim says. "What is personification?"

We watch a clip from Disney's animated *Beauty and the Beast* to show personification of teacups and candlesticks and the like, and then I end the class.

Kevin is supposed to be thinking of a sentence using an abstract noun. He comes out with "How do you cook a fish?" I write this on screen and ask him which word he thinks is an abstract noun. He says none of them, he just wants to know how to cook a fish. I ask him what this has to do with abstract nouns. He asks me again if I know about cooking fish. I tell him this is not a class about learning how to cook fish.[1]

---

1. I'm still confused by this, to be perfectly honest.

He then comes up with another sentence, in which he tells us he likes steak very much but dislikes fish. Still no abstract nouns. We rewrite it so that he has a like of steak but a dislike of fish.

However, I am left wondering why, if he dislikes fish, he needs to know how to cook them.

Friday 4 August
Number of classes: 2
Number of students: 3+1
Number of lessons to plan for Monday: 1

In today's company class with the four young boys, we instigated a new class rule: Do not cut off your head in class. Luckily, it worked, and no one did, but it always makes me nervous when students are brandishing scissors in class.

Monday 7 August
Number of classes: 2
Number of students: 3+1
Number of lessons to plan for tomorrow: 2

I explain to the class that *towards* is British English and *toward* is US English. Apple explains to me that if the sentence is **he runs towards the house,** then towards should have an **s**, but if the sentence is **I run toward the house**, it should have no **s** and I am totally impressed by her grasp of subject/verb agreement, and how she applied the logic to this, even though she is wrong about toward/towards.

I cancel Yiyi's class because I have a headache, but it wouldn't have killed me to have met her anyway. It's hardly hard work. It does mean her lesson for next week is already prepared.

Tuesday 8 August
Number of classes: 4
Number of students: 1+2+4+2
Number of lessons to plan for tomorrow: 3

Kate and Honey are supposed to have come to class with an idea of someone they would like to write a biography about. They have no idea. We try to brainstorm. They think of no one, aside from Kate suggesting she'd like to write about her friend and the time they played together.

We brainstorm some more.

It doesn't help.

I try googling famous Chinese people, Chinese singers, Chinese actors, Chinese sportspeople, and so on, hoping they may recognise one of the images.

They don't.

Honey eventually remembers Elaine Wu winning something or other in the winter Olympics, but she doesn't want to write about her.

I ask them if they can think of anyone, anyone at all, from Chinese history.

They can't.

We settle on them agreeing that they will interview their grandparents for this week's homework.

Catherine and Mango are finally, finally, done with *Wonder* and I am delighted. Except now we need to agree what to do next. Catherine's mum has suggested *Robinson Crusoe*. I have unsuggested it.

WEDNESDAY 9 AUGUST
NUMBER OF CLASSES: 3
NUMBER OF STUDENTS: 1+3+2
NUMBER OF LESSONS TO PLAN FOR TOMORROW: 1

Spring, once again, is alone in class. This turns out to be a good thing, as she really can't get to grips with a children's picture book about Henry 'Box' Brown and the history of slavery and the Underground Railroad[2]. She is seven, and this is both ancient history and foreign history to her. She can't fathom it at all. It's also our second week of this book, and I had hoped that after last week's introduction to it, she'd cope better this week. She tells me she has read the book, but still doesn't understand it. We watch videos. I explain slavery again. I explain, again, that Henry had a pretty crappy life. She doesn't understand much.

---

2. Levine, E. and Nelson, K., *Henry's Freedom Box*, Scholastic, 2007

After class, Spring's mum tells me that Spring has not, in fact, read the book.

I set Harry and Susie a writing task. Harry announces he's fed up with writing and isn't going to write a story. Fair enough.

THURSDAY 10 AUGUST
NUMBER OF CLASSES: 4
NUMBER OF STUDENTS: 1+3+2
NUMBER OF LESSONS TO PLAN FOR TOMORROW: 0

Cynthia arrives in class today with a pair of googly eyes fixed to her glasses. They stare at me throughout the lesson.

Later, Mira shows up for her class in a t-shirt with a puppet/muppet/something on – all I can focus on are its enormous googly eyes. Looking at me for the whole lesson.

Friday 11 August
Number of classes: 2
Number of students: 2+1
Number of lessons to plan for Monday: 0

Eric and Bourne are so unresponsive today I presume they must have started back at school already, but no. It's still the summer holidays, but they have been busy as ever and are too tried to do a class at 8 p.m. on a Friday night.

Sometimes I disagree so strongly with the ethics of this job, but I know if they weren't doing class with me, they'd still be doing it with someone else, so I may as well take their cash as anyone. At least I try to make the classes *fun*…

Having cancelled Yiyi's class last Monday, it's nice to go into the weekend with her Monday lesson already prepared and no work to think about over the weekend.

TUESDAY 15 AUGUST
NUMBER OF CLASSES: 4
NUMBER OF STUDENTS: 1+2+3+2
NUMBER OF LESSONS TO PLAN FOR TOMORROW: 3

I log onto my conversational platform ready to meet Dorrie, and find the platform has been 'improved' yet again. I'm still not recovered from the last lot of stupid improvements that have made teaching on this platform Hell on Earth, and this new update looks no more user friendly than the last ones. I have a message wating for me, and it's from someone I don't know. I open it, to find an answer to an earlier inquiry and response.

Here's the actual transcript of how my morning began:

28 Mar: Hi Jeanette; I hope you are doing well. I wonder do you have session with children ,10 years old.I ma asking for my daughter who is in beginer level.

28 Mar: Hello, I am quite busy at the moment, but I may have a free time on Tuesdays at 6.30pm Turkiye time. Would that work for you?

Yesterday 1:59 PM: Thanks for quickest response in advance . Tuesdays 6.30 pm perfectly fits my agenda.

9:46 AM: I sent that response in March. It is now August! I am no longer available

I also get a message from my company. Honey's mum is doubting the course, as Honey often chooses to use voice-to-text to write her stories. Honey is often anxious in class, and almost never has time to do homework, prep, or reading. In our literature classes, she has yet to read the right chapters in time for any class. She does a million other classes each week, and today, rolled into class twenty minutes late because, once again, she came straight from a ping pong lesson.

Have I any advice for her mother, I am asked.

Well, yes, indeed I have. Take some fricking pressure off this poor child. Make sure she has time to DO the preparation work for her classes. Make sure she is able to get to the class on time, fed, refreshed, and ready.

Poor child. She is a great student, but is in danger of associating learning English with stress and worry.

Wednesday 16 August
Number of classes: 3
Number of students: 1+3+1
Number of lessons to plan for tomorrow: 1

Honey, whose mother complained yesterday, is in a car today, travelling. For the few parts of the class she is connected to the internet, she is unable to get her camera to work. She is mostly unable to participate. How her mother expects her to do well in the lessons is far beyond me. How Honey does do so well is a miracle, and testament to just how hard we are all working to ensure she gets a good lesson.

Spring, still enjoying one-to-one, finds Malala Yousafzai's story[3] easier to understand than 1800s-America slavery, although her main take from Malala's story of fighting for girls' rights to education and being shot by the Taliban is that Malala wanted a magic pencil.

Thursday 17 August
Number of classes: 3
Number of students: 3+3+4
Number of lessons to plan for tomorrow: 0

Teresa, back in class for the first time in a while, spends class eating her dinner, with her mum and sister jumping around her in the background. It's so great to have her back.

Usually, this lesson is my favourite in this course and involves watching a great little animated film. However, today, Kim,

---

3. Yousafzai, M, *Malala's Magic Pencil*, Puffin, 2019

Teresa, and Luna don't like the film, don't get it, and write bugger all of any use about it for their review. I've gone off this lesson.

Alice finally shows up for her class, twelve weeks into the sixteen-week course. It's lovely to see her again though. Kevin and Orlando have both lost their work. Good thing today is the start of a new project, all things considered.

In the last class of the day, all four students show up, and all four might as well have not bothered. The content of today's class is hard for this level, and boring as heck. Luffy claims he understands it. The girls appear not to. Jolin speaks about twice, and only when reading. Even Cynthia seems to be asleep or comatose. I can't say I blame them.

Friday 18 August
Number of classes: 1
Number of students: 3
Number of lessons to plan for Monday: 1

Eric, Bourne, and Jerry are on good form and respond well and stay awake throughout the class. A definite win for this class today. Maybe I brought more of my own energy knowing it was my only class of the day!

Monday 21 August
Number of classes:
Number of students: 3+2+1
Number of lessons to plan for tomorrow: 1

Sky rocks up about twenty minutes late, and cares only about why Apple is missing.

Apple, it seems, has quit BOTH her classes, mid-course, without so much as a goodbye. We will miss her a lot, and the classes will be quieter without her. I'm taking it personally, too, as apparently 'her mother wants her to try different English classes'. Hmph.

In last Monday's literature class, I only had Xika. Today, I have Winson and Bruno. Gotta love the continuity. Luckily, the book this week is a new one, and the boys don't need to know last week's work. Unluckily, both boys are travelling, and we have to do a lot of improvising to cope with noise, movement, interruptions, and lack of pencils, notebooks, or textbooks.

Tuesday 22 August
Number of classes: 4
Number of students: 1+1+3+3
Number of lessons to plan for tomorrow: 3

Kate, alone in class today (this is how well it's going for Honey), has forgotten to bring her work, forgotten to do her work, and not spoken to her grandparents at all. We improvise the class and research Amelia Earhart, which is much more fun than the scheduled materials.

Once again, Kayley gets confused about what she is to write. She TELLS me a great sentence about what she does before she goes to bed, but then she copies the list of 'spelling words' I have written on screen instead of writing her great sentence.

Catherine and Mango cancel at short notice, and I am delighted, as I have planned their lesson and won't have to plan it next week.

I am covering some Romanian classes this week and have a joyless hour of discussing the passive voice with three uninspired 10ish-year olds.

WEDNESDAY 23 AUGUST
NUMBER OF CLASSES: 4
NUMBER OF STUDENTS: 1+3+2+6
NUMBER OF LESSONS TO PLAN FOR TOMORROW: 1

Honey has not got the book we are studying. She has an e-copy, but cannot look at that simultaneously to taking the class. Let me remind you once more that since her mother complained about the classes, Honey has been:

1. Travelling and unable to participate.
2. Absent.
3. Without the books she needs.

Harry is predictably unimpressed to be presented with a full PET practice test today, but I enjoy forty-minutes of not having to talk. They have agreed to study *The Indian in the*

Cupboard[4] next, so I spend the class time googling around the internet for resources.

In Romania, the Beginners class has moved on from the horrendous Genki classes and are doing an Oxford Phonics course. We are focusing on sounds, but they know letter names rather than sounds, and write only in capitals.

THURSDAY 24 AUGUST
NUMBER OF CLASSES: 4
NUMBER OF STUDENTS: 1+3+3+2
NUMBER OF LESSONS TO PLAN FOR TOMORROW: 0

Jolin, once again, does not speak until about forty minutes into the class, and once again, this is only to read.

In the Romanian hour, only two students arrive. I'm not surprised the others would duck out of another hour on the passive voice. As the attending two find this difficult, I pinch some materials from my Chinese lessons and give them a far easier intro to passive voice than their own class materials give.

---

4. Reid banks, L, *The Indian in the Cupboard*, Harper Collins, 1988

At least, *I* understand it better by the time we are done, even if they don't.

F ## Friday 25 August
Number of classes: 2
Number of students: 2+4+6
Number of lessons to plan for Monday: 1

Lindsey and Iris's class finally restarts. Iris, predictably, is late. I am not convinced persuading her to start up classes again was the best idea I ever had. She also switches back and forth between devices, resulting in her mother calling me on a voice call in the middle of class to demand I restart the class so Iris can rejoin. Iris, meanwhile, has already rejoined, but can only connect on her phone, not her iPad... It has also been so long since their last class that I remembered wrongly where we had got to and start in the wrong place. In better news, Lindsey shows me her holiday snaps while we wait for Iris to sort herself out, and now I want to go to the hot springs for a week.

In the teen group, we skip almost all the grammar in the section they are supposed to be working on, because I have no idea what it is talking about. *Reduced restrictive clauses* or some such madness. Whatever they are[5], we collectively decide to skip to the next Ted talk and leave the grammar stuff for John (the teacher I'm covering for).

MONDAY 28 AUGUST
NUMBER OF CLASSES: 3
NUMBER OF STUDENTS: 2+3+2
NUMBER OF LESSONS TO PLAN FOR TOMORROW: 0

I wake to a message reminding me that Sean will attend today's literature class. Sean has great vocabulary, conversational skills, and knowledge, but he is only four, maybe five by now, and the content of the books we study is far above his age group. Today's class is the second lesson about a slavery text (*Henry's Freedom Box*), and next week we venture into child marriage and shooting by the Taliban as we study *Malala's Magic Pencil* and an accompanying piece about Payal Jangid. While these are important topics, I'm not sure a four-year-old needs to study these just yet, especially in a second language.

---

5. I've been spotting them in reading ever since.

Sky, meanwhile, proves to have great knowledge of women's issues in his class. We open with a warm-up question on who they have helped today. Sky informs us that his mum is sick today, and he knows that women have something each month that makes them feel ill, so he did his mum's washing and took her breakfast in bed and my heart is warm and full.

My worries about Sean were founded. He thinks Henry from Henry's Freedom Box didn't like living in Africa, so he put himself in the box to escape, but moreover, Sean can't write in English yet, and a large part of these classes involves writing. Having him in this class will entirely negate the point of bumping Rain out of the class. Xika, who missed last week's lesson, which I have forgotten, doesn't at any point remind me of this, or tell me that no, she knows none of the background either. Only now I write this do I even realise that she was absent last week.

Three-year-old Xiaorou stays around for much of Yiyi's lesson today, and delights us all by saying "spaceman" as clear as anything, despite not saying much else through the entire class.

Tuesday 29 August
Number of classes: 4
Number of students: 1+2+3+2
Number of lessons to plan for tomorrow: 2

Dorrie has dropped her two 30-minute classes a week down to one 30-minute lesson, and the difference in her reading is noticeable. Since I want to drop this conversational platform anyway, and only have Dorrie and Mira left on it, I won't email her mum to tell her that she's really missing out from reducing the hours. Besides, she's got too much else on, with starting high school tomorrow, but it does kind of prove the point that the more you speak a language, the easier it is. She is making so many reading mistakes that she hadn't made in ages it's as if we've gone back a year or so.

Catherine and Mango start *The Boy Who Lived in the Ceiling*[6] today, and although it was my suggestion (after rejecting all Catherine's mum's horrendous ideas and her rejecting all my easier ones), I have a lot of reservations as it's still above-level and I think it's going to be a long drag like *Wonder* was, despite being another great book. They have

---

6. Thurlbourn, C., *The Boy who Lived in the Ceiling*, Wise Wolf Books, 2021

become very unresponsive since Catherine's mum insisted we tackle these heavier, older texts that are too old for them in both knowledge and English level.

WEDNESDAY 30 AUGUST
NUMBER OF CLASSES: 2
NUMBER OF STUDENTS: 1+2
NUMBER OF LESSONS TO PLAN FOR TOMORROW: 1

Spring has her class alone *again* today. Next week this class will merge with the Monday class and Spring will repeat the two lessons on Malala Yousafzai. She struggles with today's lesson, not least because she doesn't understand what child marriage is and our comparative text is about Payal Jangid. It's not easy explaining the idea of child marriage to a seven-year-old who doesn't really understand the idea in her own language, never mind in a second language.

In Susie and Harry's lesson, we start *The Indian in the Cupboard* and I hadn't realised just how much 'big' language is in it. I've downloaded a zillion lesson plans, but the main one – about an inch thick, that I have printed out – is geared towards much older students and some of the language in the lesson is even more complex than the language in the book. Harry, who knows the story, is at a noisy party and has bad internet connection too, which does at least give Susie a lot of time to focus on questions one-to-one.

THURSDAY 31 AUGUST
NUMBER OF CLASSES: 3
NUMBER OF STUDENTS: 4+4+4
NUMBER OF LESSONS TO PLAN FOR TOMORROW: 0

Today is the final class of the course for Kim, Luna, Teresa, Evelyn. Remarkably, all four show up.

Kim, after our tricky start ages ago when I first met him, has become a pleasure to teach and is great classmate now. Teresa, meanwhile, has gone the other way – she tries, she really does, but with non-stop noise and her mother interfering in class, the poor girl hasn't a chance. As usual, she spends more of the class being muted, to drown out her mother and sister, than not.

In the second class of the day, all four students also turn up. The summer holidays are clearly over. They've also all done their homework, and we know more about Einstein than I ever knew I needed to know. We've come up with some new questions for them to research before next week, because it's clearly crucial to know how tall he was.

> **Albert Einstein**
> **Important life events**
>
> **What have you learned?**
> Compare your notes and decide what else you need to find out.
>
> Let's find out more about:
>
> What else he liked to play. Who did he play with? Where did he play?
>
> Why did he like to play violin? Did he like other music?
>
> Which schools did he go to?
>
> How did he do in tests in school?
>
> How tall was he?
>
> When did he invent E=MC2?
>
> Did he get married? Did he have children?
>
> I can select only the most important events in my subject's life to include in a biography.
>
> Writers select only the most important parts of a person's life to write about so that their readers will understand why the person is important
>
> The Most Important Events:
> 1.
> 2.
> 3.
> 4.
> 5.
> 6.
> 7.
> 8.
> 9.
> 10.

Full House! I end the month with a hat trick, as in the third class, also all four students show up. Luffy is not as silly in this class as he used to be and I have to admit, I kind of miss it. Jolin, as usual, answers no questions. I only know she is there because she reads from the onscreen text when asked.

September

FRIDAY 1 SEPTEMBER
NUMBER OF CLASSES: 1
NUMBER OF STUDENTS: 4
NUMBER OF LESSONS TO PLAN FOR MONDAY: 1

Lindsey and Iris have postponed, so it's an easy, one-class day, although having just one class in the very middle of a day (1 P.M. British Summer Time) is a pain in the arse, too.

For what feels like the eleventy-millionth time, we go over **us** versus **use**. I'm not entirely sure Jerry will ever get the difference, and Sean and Bourne are pretty mush asleep by now, so we don't make much progress.

MONDAY 4 SEPTEMBER
NUMBER OF CLASSES: 2
NUMBER OF STUDENTS: 3+4
NUMBER OF LESSONS TO PLAN FOR TOMORROW: 0

Iris's mum has asked to swap days.

Yiyi has had a nasty fall so her mum cancels class at the last minute. I am already in class, but not ready for it, as I haven't quite finished preparing the lesson. I'm relieved for the cancellation, and now the bulk of the lesson is well-ready for next Monday instead.

TUESDAY 5 SEPTEMBER
NUMBER OF CLASSES: 4
NUMBER OF STUDENTS: 1+2+3+2
NUMBER OF LESSONS TO PLAN FOR TOMORROW: 0

Turned out swapping classes around was easy, and the bonus is that I now don't have to plan anything for Tuesday's classes, as all the lessons are ones I've taught before. Iris and Lindsey's lesson goes surprisingly well, with minimal interruptions from Iris's mother, and no internet problems. Looks like Tuesdays will suit these girls.

WEDNESDAY 6 SEPTEMBER
NUMBER OF CLASSES: 3
NUMBER OF STUDENTS: 2+3+2
NUMBER OF LESSONS TO PLAN FOR TOMORROW: I

Today doesn't get off to a great start.

Me (at 10:54 A.M., which is precisely six minutes before the class start time): *Hi, I just realised (very late!!!) I don't have any of the info for the trial class - no Zoom number AND No lesson file. I'm so sorry, I though I had GKB Reading on file but it's vanished!*

Fiona: *lesson file on the way*

Fiona: *dealing now*

Me: *Thanks! I am so sorry to be unprepared - I was so certain I had it!*

Fiona: *easy*

Fiona: *solving*

Me: *Thank you!*

She sends the class code.

A moment later:
Fiona: *i need 5 minutes*
Me: *Me too!!! But I am in the classroom, so we will be fine...*

And it was. Jessica and Yuwei were great and worked well together.[1]

In the second class, Honey, Sophia, and Natalie are as lovely as ever. My regular Wednesday breath of fresh air.

Harry and Susie bring the same old same old. An easy class, with easy chat. I love these two. I love Wednesdays. (Aside from the early panic of today.)

THURSDAY 7 SEPTEMBER
NUMBER OF CLASSES: 3
NUMBER OF STUDENTS: 2+3+1
NUMBER OF LESSONS TO PLAN FOR TOMORROW: 1

Today's warm up poses the question: *What would you do if you found a magic wand.*

---

1. I never saw them again.

Kevin, uncharacteristically sensible, would throw it away, wary of its powers.

Nimo, menacingly, would use his lucky find to wipe out most of China. First he would eliminate all the men. He'd keep the women, initially, to have babies. Then, he'd kill off all the women too. Not a bit scary, Nimo. Not a bit.

I'm on Team Orlando for the magic wand idea – use it to get billions of dollars, but still somewhat impressed by Kevin's cautious wisdom.

In the later class, Jolin starts out well, for a nice change, and responds to some questions, but then partway through the class, she reverts to type and only speaks when it's her turn to read. It's hard to know how much she understands when she refuses to participate. Cynthia and Luffy are out of patience, and even when I do try to give Jolin time to respond, one of her classmates will quickly decide they can't wait any longer, and give the answer for her.

FRIDAY 8 SEPTEMBER
NUMBER OF CLASSES: 2
NUMBER OF STUDENTS: 2+4
NUMBER OF LESSONS TO PLAN FOR MONDAY: 1

I'd hoped that meeting Mango and Catherine at an earlier time might make them chattier. It doesn't. I am cursing myself for having let myself be talked into another book that is beyond their ability. By the end of the class, my voice has almost gone, and I still have another class to get through.

Sean, in the boys' class, has decided to answer most personal small-talk questions with "I'm not going to tell you," which makes me think his parents have told him to give away absolutely no personal information in case I try to hack his bank account or something.

Monday 11 September
Number of classes: 3
Number of students: 1+2+3+2
Number of lessons to plan for tomorrow: 0

The first class today goes surprisingly easily. Everyone participates well and they aren't even daunted by the Spanish words in today's text. If only Sky and Jessica would sort out the horrendous echo on their devices, we'd be laughing, but instead, despite an easy and enjoyable class, I have a headache from the constant buzz and noise.

Although Kayley brings almost every animal we ever mention to class – today it is a frog and a turtle, and once again, I find myself urging a student to please, please, not squeeze their pets so hard — and she can tell us lots about the spider in the picture onscreen, she still can't write a complete sentence. Her first attempt is ***A eight leg and eat fly.***[2]

I say this has good ideas but is not a full sentence, and write the sentence correctly: ***A spider had eight legs and eats flies.***

---

2. I have to admit, I kind of love this description, and A Eight Leg and Eat Fly was a strong contender for the title of this book.

Kayley simply adds more to her original effort: ***A eight leg and eat fly. and black.***

She's really not getting the whole "here's what you must write, look, I've written it for you to copy" idea. I am increasingly certain she might be dyslexic, and have raised this with the company several times to no response.

In other news, I sometimes get materials from sites where teachers make and sell their efforts. The company I work for does this too. Many of these materials are riddled with mistakes, usually spelling or grammar, but today's spider worksheet feels like an all-time low. The illustrated spider, though cute and smiling, has only six legs. I always begin this lesson by getting someone to draw on the extras.

Yiyi is doing well! She is remembering so many words now, and even got Chip's name right every time.[3] Beginners are always so happy!

---

3. As in Biff, Chip, and Kipper, from the Oxford Reading Tree series, by Roderick Hunt and Alex Brychta, Oxford University Press.

Tuesday 12 September
Number of classes: 34
Number of students: 1+2+3+2
Number of lessons to plan for tomorrow: 2

I wake this morning to a string of requests to juggle the company classes around. I think they forgot I wouldn't be answering at 3 A.M. my time. We are switching the Thursday 6 P.M. class to Thursday 8 P.M., and the Thursday 8 P.M. to Friday 6 P.M., but not this Friday as I've other things planned.

The students who did last Wednesday's trial can't do any more classes at that time, which begs the question why trial at that time? More than anything, this rearranging of classes proves school has started again for all my students. Their tiredness reiterates that fact.

Iris, despite having insisted on changing the day, is late. Once again, her mother sends me a screenshot of what I presume is a message telling her she can't get into the classroom. It's in Chinese, so I can only guess what it says. As usual, in the exact moment she sent the message, Iris pops up in class. The problem seems to be not with the classroom, but with the device she uses to log on. The rest of the class passes easily enough, aside from a message from Mango's mum, asking if the class has started.

We switched to Friday, remember. I remind her.
Oh yes. she replies.
I predict similar fun on Friday.

WEDNESDAY 13 SEPTEMBER
NUMBER OF CLASSES: 3
NUMBER OF STUDENTS: 3+2+1
NUMBER OF LESSONS TO PLAN FOR TOMORROW: 1

A new trial student called Yudi is to come to our Literature class. I'm not delighted, as this class is perfect with Honey, Sophia and Natalie, and is my favourite class each week. A new student would surely spoil that balance and vibe.

An hour and a half after the class ends, I realise Yudi didn't show up. Oops.

Thursday 14th September
Number of classes: 3
Number of students: 3+2+1
Number of lessons to plan for tomorrow: 1

A nice quiet day with only two of the usual three company classes. They have switched around this week, and the usual 6 p.m. class is now at 8 p.m., and the usual 8 p.m. is moving to next Friday instead.

In the first class, neither Kevin nor Orlando have bothered to do or bring their Einstein work to class. Alice and Craig, who have missed most of the course, have both done the work. Alice, luckily, had brought hers to the previous lesson too, and I have a copy of it, as today she is at first skating, then in a car, then somewhere else and then somewhere else, and we can't hear a word she says.

Friday 15th September
Number of classes: 1
Number of students: 4
Number of lessons to plan for Monday: 1

What should have been two classes today has dropped to one, as Catherine, newly bumped to Friday to make way for Lindsey and Iris on Tuesday, has flu. I'm sad for her, of course, but delighted too. It's my husband's birthday and also my daughter's last day at home before leaving to start a new job in another country at the crack of dawn tomorrow. I get through my one class in much the usual way we get through that class, except no one falls asleep today.

Monday 18th September
Number of classes: 2
Number of students: 3+4
Number of lessons to plan for tomorrow: 0

I do a bad thing and cancel Yiyi's class. I have kittens to collect, instead.

Tuesday 19th September
Number of classes: 4
Number of students: 1+1+
Number of lessons to plan for tomorrow: 2

Dorrie is only slightly interrupted by my dogs barking at escaped kittens. They are supposed to be shut in the utility room, but have got through the catflap. Sam – my smaller dog – is unimpressed and barks incessantly. Wilf, wanting to play, almost pulls my arm off as I hold him by his collar and try to focus on *Harry Potter* and Dorrie's lesson.

Honey is absent from her class again, so Kate and I enjoy another one-to-one class. Her story is both good, and boring. She has had a good idea for her fantasy story, in which a girl finds a magic pencil. The magic pencil breaks – clarified as "running out because the girl drew too much" – but the girl simply buys a new one. Rinse and repeat. I sing Kate a little snippet of *The Bear Climbed Over The Mountain* to prove the point, and Kate is now working on a more exciting plot twist.

And then what happened?

Here, the day after the kittens arrive, the diary abruptly stops. It wasn't just about the kittens, I promise.

I had, in July, after completing my MA, made a crucial decision regarding some of my novels and decided to self-publish my cozy mystery series, otherwise, following the brief stint of what turned out to be a Bad Publishing Experience with Book 1, the rest of the series would be unlikely to see the light of day.

Why I didn't even complete the record for the 19th September, I have no idea. Perhaps the last two classes were horrendous. I could check old records to see. A mix of the information on my calendar and my class feedback files would give me all the clues I'd need. It was a Tuesday, so I know it included my most difficult class. I expect Kayley left me on the edge of tears, insanity, or drink. I probably went off for a long lie-down, swearing I'd never teach again.

Yet, here I am. Heading fast towards the end of 2025 and still teaching ESL alongside writing my novels; still loving it.

Since September 2023, I have changed companies. The company I had been working for folded, which was a real shame. You might have noticed the classes slowly dropping off my schedule. I hadn't minded too much, as I was frantically trying to meet MA and book deadlines. However, I loved the students and I loved the communication I had with my Chinese coordinators, and I especially loved the freedom they gave me to cater each class to the students.

For the last few months with that lovely little company, I could see the end coming. I really hoped it wouldn't, but it seemed inevitable; the company had stopped renewing students' courses once their current course ended, and by Christmas 2023, I was down to just three company classes a week, and with the founder absent (overseas, working on an MA and then a PHD – we've stayed in touch) her mostly-unpaid staff hadn't the incentive to continue. Aside from everything else, that particular company also paid better than any company I've worked for before or since. While that went a very long way to my job satisfaction, I imagine it also went some way to the company not surviving.

I still have some of the same private students. Yiyi is now seven, and still brings happiness to every class. Xiaorou pops in from time-to-time but rarely stays for the whole lesson. Susie and Iris now have one-to-one classes, and even though Harry and Lindsey stopped due to pressures of school, we stay in touch. I also hear from Amy from time to time, and she sends photos to which I usually respond with that old cliché – hasn't she got tall!

I also found new students very quickly, through a new company, and continued teaching without a break. Unfortunately, the new company pays a significantly lower hourly rate. Still, the students are fun, the work reasonably straightforward, and it brings me enough funny moments to prompt another diary. (Mumu alone could fill a diary. He often has class four times a week, so there are plenty of conversations to pick from.) We'll see how that goes, as I am busy enough with my fiction books, but I know there's plenty more anecdotes just begging to be shared.

Meanwhile, it's back to the juggle of writing, teaching, and creating lesson plans. If only the European Onion could help.

For anyone still wondering about the *two truths, one lie* I referred to in the introduction, the story about the student in the men's toilet in a Korean nightclub is true. The stripping grandmother reflected in the mirror? Also true. Jacob's little brother toppling a bookcase? Not quite true. He climbed the shelves often. I always thought they might fall, and peppered Jacob's and Cat's classes with calling out warnings to Jacob's little brother, but on my watch, at least, the shelves never fell.

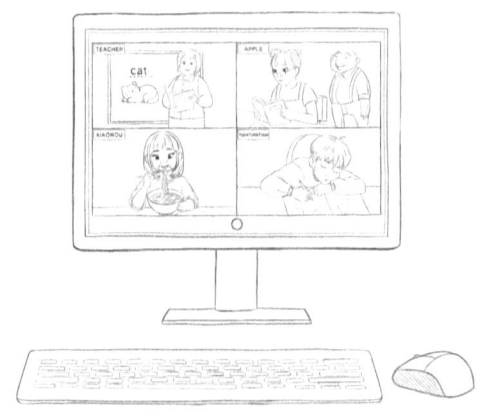

Seventy-four Days in Wuhan

Note: This short story was based on my fly-on-wall view of a six-year-old Chinese student's family, living in a small apartment in Wuhan through the Covid lockdown in the spring of 2020. A 300-word version of this story was long-listed in the prestigious Bath Flash Fiction Award in 2022.

Seventy Four Days in Wuhan

The walls creep in to meet you. The door tightens in its frame. The windows, once large enough to let the outside in, shrink with every day that passes. They are no longer your view; you can't see past their barrier. You should be out this week, far beyond that glass, celebrating with colour and light with the brightest of reds everywhere you turn. You should be squished-up travelling on an over-crowded train, rattling into countryside with pent-up, fractious children. You wouldn't mind their angst; you'd know the end was in sight. You should be hurtling towards your hometown and the holidays.

Not this year.

You'd be forgiven for ignoring the festival, but you'll do it for the children. So you mix paste for the wrappers, roll that dough as thin as the window glass used to be three weeks ago before it thickened, imperceptibly, while the walls slunk inwards. The elder child wants to help until he doesn't. His itching fingers stretch a hole in that dumpling wrapper and you'll need to start over. Spicy pork-with-chilli clambers into your nose and stings your eyes. You rub the tears and drag the boy screaming to the washroom to sponge sticky gloop from his fingers before they touch his sister's hair. You remind him again that this is temporary, necessary, and will be over soon.

It isn't.

As February limps into March, blurs into April rushing towards May, the air becomes clammy. The odour of clumsy re-made New Year dumplings has long given way to the freshly-woken, hair-plastering, sweet sweat of the smaller child mixing with the curtain-hanging, wall-climbing, bed-jumping energy of a boy who must play *somewhere*.

Your children buzz like mosquitoes on a street dog.

Through the thick, thick glass of the windows, you peer into other prisons. None are within reach. The ceiling of your apartment is lower than it used to be. Heavier. And lighter. A neighbour paces above you. Treading softly, so softly, he steps on your every remaining nerve. The miniscule, millimetres-wide stretch of almost-outside that you once thought was a balcony is too high for escape.

Or just high enough.

It doesn't cling to anyone else's balcony, so the only possibility it offers is down. Clear, clean air beckons you towards the ground. Thirteen floors down, the dim sum cart-sized empty space is the exact size to fit your tumbling body. You'd probably prefer the exhaust-filled, fume-ridden smog of *before* blinding your fall. Behind you, the baby cries. You pick her up and hold her close, thinking of elsewhere.

The seventy-fourth day is the day you break free. Your children spill into the street like a tipped-up bag of sugar, sweet, sticky, and everywhere all at once. Then, for a moment, the boy stills. Turns his face to the sky, inhales the wonder of *outside* and your heart sings for him again.

Acknowledgements

Thank you, reader, for picking up this book. It's one thing to write books, but quite another to know they are being read!

Also, of course, I thank every student featured in these pages, and their parents and the companies I work for or have have worked for in the past for entrusting me with their children's English learning experience. I love this job and am forever grateful for my students and classes. I especially love how much inspiration they give me, not only in their determination and ability, but also as an endless source of cultural insight and ideas for stories and characters in my fiction books.

I am always humbled and honoured to be invited into their homes, albeit through the magic of video conferencing, and to have these families share a part of their lives with me. I have known some of these children for years, and have loved watching them grow up as much I have enjoyed seeing their English go from "a eight leg and eat fly" or "the dragon is litagud" to fluent conversations, detailed debates, or long, written essays. Teaching across the world, from the comfort of my spare room, has given me a gift of exploring many new places and making many new friends. One day, I hope I will be able to take up some of the many invitations to visit my students and their families for real.

My students, even those who are hard work, are amazing. Every single one of them.

About the author

Jinny was first published in Horse and Pony magazine at the age of ten. She's striving to achieve equal accolades now she's (allegedly) a grown-up. Jinny has had some publishing success with short story and flash competitions and has been listed or placed in several prestigious writing contests. She has also been published in MsLexia Magazine and Writing Magazine, among other publishing credits. In 2023, Jinny completed an MA in Creative Writing with the University of Hull, for which she was awarded a Distinction.

In December 2020, Jinny secured a publishing deal for her first three novels, of which *A Diet of Death* was her second and *A Hover of Trout* the third. In 2022, Jinny reclaimed the rights to those works and continued the series. Since then, she has written several new novels, including the first in the Mrs Smith's Suspects series. This ESL diary is her first non-fiction book.

Jinny teaches English as a foreign language to people all over the world and finds her students a constant source of inspiration, for both life and stories. Her home, for now, is in rural Ireland, which she shares with her husband and far too many animals. Her two children have grown and flown, but return across the Irish Sea when they can. She likes to shut the door on them all, and write.

Also by Jinny Alexander

Jinny is the author of The Jess O'Malley Irish Village mysteries and the Mrs Smith's Suspects cozy mystery series. The second in the Mrs Smith's Suspects series will be released in 2025. The fifth Jess O'Malley book, *A Snapshot of Murder*, will follow soon.

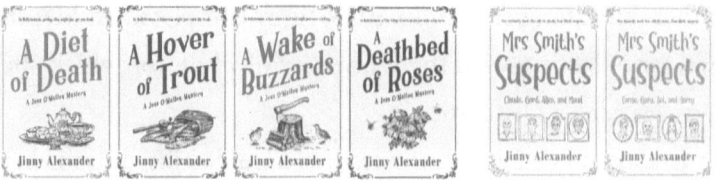

Dear Isobel (March 2022, Creative James Media) is currently out of print following Jinny's reversion of rights.

For up-to-date news and exclusive content, please sign up for Jinny's newsletter via her website: www.jinnyalexander.com

Say hello at facebook.com/JinnyAlexanderAuthor

www.ingramcontent.com/pod-product-compliance
Lightning Source LLC
Chambersburg PA
CBHW030315080526
44584CB00012B/576